ATROPOS PRESS
new york • dresden

To Paulina, having
It is great
you in my class.
you are a great
thinker!

2/18/2020

To Vrinda, and of course, my family.

The Ethics of Uncertainty
Aporetic Openings

Michael Anker

© 2009 by Michael Anker

Think Media EGS Series is supported by the European Graduate School

ATROPOS PRESS
New York • Dresden

US: 151 First Avenue # 14, New York, N.Y. 10003
Germany: Mockritzer Str. 6, D-01219 Dresden

cover design: Hannes Charen

ISBN 978-0-9748534-2-0

Contents

Part 1: Introduction

1.1 Conceptual Considerations: A Philosophical "Empirico-Materialist"[1] Strategy

In *The Puppet and the Dwarf* and other writings, Slavoj Zizek critiques (negatively, and at times for valid reasons) the "theological dimension" at work in various degrees in certain postmodern, poststructuralist, and deconstructive philosophies. He points us, of course, to the high level of interest in the "messianic" structure of time, and the interest in the "other" as a primary reference to ethics, or, as he says, an "openness toward a radical Otherness beyond the ontotheological God."[2] Any thinking on the "other" of course entails an analysis of such terms as responsibility, decision, difference, *différance*, alterity, and so on. Furthermore, a philosophical analysis of "messianic" time cannot help but investigate such notions as "to-come,"[3] (*a venir*) deferral, openings, spacing, etc., and the various ways in which a reconfigured temporal and spatial organization reorients ones relation to the world. In short, my topic "The Ethics of Uncertainty" takes up many, if not all, of these terms just mentioned. With this in mind, and with extreme emphasis, I wish to point out from the beginning, that there is no attempted "theological dimension" at work in my philosophical critique or analysis. I also do not believe, nor do I think they are Zizek's

---

[1] The empiricism implied in this term is one indebted to the philosophy of Nietzsche, John Dewey, and Gilles Deleuze. Dewey's "philosophy of experience" is not directly touched upon throughout this essay, but it stands as a constant shadowing reference and influence. It is interesting to see that Dewey's philosophy is rarely placed in connection with Continental philosophy, for as I see it, there are many productive parallels to be found. In the future, I plan to trace out these parallels and hopefully bring Dewey's thinking into a space for reconsideration.

[2] Slavoj Zizek, *The Puppet and the Dwarf*, Short Circuits (Cambridge: MIT Press, 2003), p. 5.

[3] I will frequently use this term ("to come") in different contexts ("philosophy to come," "thinking to come," "ethics to come," etc.) throughout the essay. Please note that I am always using or utilizing (in some form or another) the term in relation to Derrida's thinking on this concept. See section 2.2 for a more detailed analysis of Derrida's thinking on and in relation to this term "to come" (*a venir*).

direct target, that the philosophy of Jacques Derrida or Jean-Luc Nancy (both of whom are prominent thinkers throughout my analysis) should be read under the constraint of any "theological" underpinnings. In fact, any reading of their works which attempts to impose a theological slant or dogma over their various philosophical gestures, I believe, severely limits the political, ethical, and "of this world" impact in their thinking. In short, I believe that along with such thinkers as Zizek, who adamantly profess their materialist philosophy, Derrida and Nancy can be read and philosophically understood on a strictly materialist basis. What does this mean? It means that each and every term ("other," *différance*, openings, spacing, "to-come," aporia, becoming, etc.) finds its utmost potential for meaning and sense located around principles pertaining to the physical and material world as such. In an empirical sense, I believe we can gain ultimate insight into these concepts not only by thinking them, but by thinking them first and foremost through how we experience them in this world (temporally, spatially, etc.). Any time there is discussion on seemingly transcendental, theological, or metaphysical concepts that exceed or exist outside this world, it is easy to show that these terms are of structural importance within the world – in an ontological, phenomenological, or epistemological framework. Many of the "theological" concepts used throughout their work (and in this essay) function as structural or exemplary tools for analysis and enunciation of worldly matters in the form of ethics and politics. Metaphorically speaking, perhaps one could describe the phenomena of using theological terms for materialist purposes as a type of topology[4] where a shift occurs not (originally) in the meaning (point) of the term, but in the reconfigured space. In other words, the shift in meaning occurs not *a priori* its point of theoretical departure from theology, but only possibly afterward in the new contextual (in this case materialist) space of configuration. An example of this, and there are many more

---

[4] It would be interesting to analyze conceptual topologies in such a way as to mark the various shifts in meaning (point) *after* a movement into a newly configured or contextual space. In other words, how much does the meaning of a concept change *after* its move, for example, from one realm of thought to another?

which will be analyzed throughout this essay, is Derrida's thinking on a "messianicity without messianism."[5] Once again, throughout this essay all attempts are made to veer away from a thinking which attempts an alignment of thought outside (transcendentally, metaphysically) the world as such – world as world, world as absolutely nothing other than world. Here, with the words of Jean-Luc Nancy, we could say that our thinking will remain focused on a "sense of the world" where "world is the spacing of sense."[6] For Nancy, there is no outside the world – world is sense and sense is world. But all of this for us is not a limitation; it is a pure opening for thought in and of our being and becoming in this world. The world as such, world simply as world, is always already in absolute excess of itself in differentiation. This movement of difference is already there, already happening, for as Derrida would say, difference itself already exists within attempted unity. This differentiating movement within the world creates a constant play and transformation – a continuous spacing which opens the world to novelty and event. In short, the world in itself *is* enough.

As a final thought on this issue, it is interesting to note that in one of Zizek's most recent books entitled *The Parallax View*, he seems to steer his critique away from Derrida and more toward thinkers who have perhaps misinterpreted or misappropriated Derrida's philosophical use of theological concepts and terminology. In relation to this issue and after stating the importance of understanding the notion "minimal difference" in relation to his overall thesis on the "parallax gap," Zizek states:

> Since I have written many pages in which I struggle with the work of Jacques Derrida, now – when the Derridean fashion is fading away – is perhaps the moment to honor his memory by pointing out the proximity of this "minimal difference" to what he called *différance*, this neologism whose very notoriety obfuscates its

---

[5] Jacques Derrida, "Faith and Knowledge," in *Religion*, ed. Jacques Derrida and Gianni Vattimo (Stanford: Stanford University Press, 1998), p. 17. There are also numerous other texts by Derrida which discuss this conceptual construct.
[6] See appendix

unprecedented materialist potential. If anything,
however, this reappraisal is intended to draw an
even stronger line of demarcation from the usual
gang of democracy-to-come-deconstructionist-
postsecular-Levinasian-respect-for-Otherness
suspects.[7]

So I ask the reader once again to keep in mind that my intentions
are not to follow the "democracy-to-come-deconstructionist-
postsecular-Levinasian-respect-for-Otherness" gang of thinkers,
but more so to follow a trajectory which always remains faithful
to an empirical materialist "in this world" philosophy for
politics, being/becoming, and ethics.   The power of Zizek's
thinking is in his constant reminder of how easy it is (if not
careful) to fall prey to a style of thinking which leads not only to
a "theological dimension" in thought, but to a type of thinking
which leads to a constant deferral without a dimension of active
decision.   As you will see throughout this essay, I believe
Derrida, Nancy, and perhaps most thoroughly the philosophy of
Wolfgang Schirmacher[8] (along with my overall critique on
aporetic openings in relation to uncertainty) provide a clear
move or temporary passage (*poros*) out of the antinomies we
face in a world without predetermined meanings or absolute
measure.   In fact, I believe along with Derrida, that it is only
possible to live up to such things as responsibility and decision if
one first "endures the aporia" or "double bind" which precedes,
maintains, and follows any act of determinacy.   I say
"maintains" in the sense of upholding the aporetic "structure"

---

[7] Slavoj Zizek, *The Parallax View*, Short Circuits (Cambridge: MIT Press, 2006),
p. 11.
[8] My essay does not attempt a full analysis of Schirmacher's philosophy, but I
believe his work offers valuable insight into how one can live, decide, and
perhaps even live an "ethical" life in a world without absolute measure.   In
chapter 4.6 we will look briefly at his philosophy of "homo generator" and
"imperceptible fulfillment."   Overall, his thinking points to a type of affirmative
existence, an affirmation of being and becoming outside the metaphysics of
certainty and absolute truth as a guide.   In this sense, homo generator (in
becoming) generates within the context of a thoroughly contextual world.   In
doing so, homo generator also creates new contexts for him/her self in an
inventive yet "imperceptible" manner.

and not allowing the momentary decision to become totalized and thus closed off from once again new possibilities, and I say "follows" in the sense that immediately after a decision is made, it is necessary to once again fold back into the uncertain space for a new thinking to come. Of course what precedes any true decision is not knowledge or certainty, but the "undecidability" (Derrida) within decidability. But we will have plenty more to say on this as we move on. For now, it is important to keep in mind the "empirico-materialist" strategy I have in mind as we move through at times a seemingly "theological" terrain of thinking on/with Derrida, Nancy, and others. Even more so, I hope, and in agreement with Zizek, to not only unleash the "materialist potential" in Derrida's notion of *différance*, but of all such notions utilized for a thinking on ethics, politics, and the becoming of being in and with this world as such. All in all, and stated in concise terms, there is a "empirico-materialist" strain in the tradition of Nietzsche, Dewey, and Deleuze, which runs as an undercurrent through all my thinking and in particular, the work at hand. The next section will not only exemplify this point, but furthermore position this empirico-materialist strategy within the context of thinking on aporetic openings and all that this entails.

1.2 A Precursor to Aporetic Openings: The Movement of Becoming

> As something is coming to be it is always already becoming something other.[9]

The above passage (statement?) represents, by way of summarization, a continued thought in relation to a trajectory of thinkers from Heraclitus, Nietzsche, Heidegger, Deleuze, and in a more contemporary setting, a particular aspect in the philosophy of Derrida, Nancy, and Schirmacher. I do not mean to suggest here that these philosophers in any way think *only*

---

[9] The statement is an attempt to summarize or paraphrase a particular element of thinking on becoming in relation to such philosophers as Heraclitus to Derrida and others.

according to this conceptual construct, but more so that this statement on continuous becoming sits as a type of undercurrent to their respective philosophies. In regard to its relation to Heraclitus, this is of course quite obvious. In the philosophy of Nietzsche, we can find elements of this statement perhaps everywhere, but in particular in his thinking on the "will to power." With Heidegger, we can see various connections, but most importantly in *Dasein*, *Mitsein*, and the phenomenological notion of simultaneous revealing and concealing. Deleuze, of course, in allegiance with Nietzsche's thinking amongst others, orients his "rhizomatic" philosophy in an unfolding/folding movement of continuous becoming. As for Derrida, Nancy, and Schirmacher, the essay at hand will hopefully show. For now, however, I will suggest that a correlation exists primarily in Derrida's notion of *différance*, Nancy's "sense" of "being singular plural," and in Schirmacher's formulation of "homo generator." In all the above mentioned, I find a relation to thinking which corresponds to the phrase, "as something is coming to be it is always already becoming something other."

The above mentioned phrase, therefore, will also serve as a prominent undercurrent to many of the ideas which follow throughout this essay. The phrase by itself opens the space for a type of thinking on ontology, phenomenology, epistemology, psychology, ethics, and politics. Each of these realms or conceptual domains for thinking about the world, are somewhat at play in relation to the statement. The meaning asks for consideration from each of these fields – it asks each of them to consider the reverberations of a world in passing, a transience of being without origin, without measure, and without totalized unity. But before we look toward the reverberations, let us look closer at the statement or phrase in itself. For the sake of clarity, I have listed ten possible meanings which come to the surface. There are obviously more, but for our purposes, those listed below will suffice.

In relation to "as something is coming to be it is always already becoming something other":

1. There is only continuous activity, motion, movement, change, and transformation.

Of emphasis here is the affirmation that there is no outside or transcendental, unconditional, timeless space untouched by the transformations of the material world. The world is continuous activity and becoming, or, here we could make use of Nietzsche's concept of "will to power," in particular his description of the world as will to power in the final aphorism (1067) of the collection of writings published as "Will to Power."[10] For Nietzsche, there are only *relations of force* which make up the movements and motion of the world. It is also helpful here to think of this space of on-going motion, as a type of Deleuzian plateau with rhizomatic characteristics. As Deleuze states in regard to a rhizome, "It is composed not of units but of dimensions, or rather directions *in motion* (emphasis mine)."[11]

2. There is a simultaneous action – an "at the same time" occurrence.

Of importance here is the recognition that there is not a simple causal chain at work where some-thing merely leads to an-other thing and so on, but in the continuous activity some-thing is always already some-thing other. In short, there is no clear line of demarcation which separates the cause from the effect; they are simultaneously caught up in both, or perhaps we could say neither. Here it would be useful to look at Nietzsche's constant deconstruction of the notions cause and effect in "On the Genealogy of Morals." Also, again with Deleuze's rhizomatic philosophy of becoming, we can recognize a non-linear trajectory of transformation when he states that a rhizome "has neither beginning nor end, but always a middle (milieu) from which it grows and which it overspills."[12]

---

[10] Friedrich Nietzsche, *The Will to Power*, trans. Walter Kaufman and R.J. Hollingdale (New York: Vintage Books, 1968), pp. 549-550.
[11] Gilles Deleuze, and Felix Guattari, *A Thousand Plateaus* (Minneapolis: University of Minnesota Press, 1987), p. 21.
[12] Ibid

3. There is a temporal/spatial relationship between being and becoming.

In short, being and becoming are one and the same gesture. Being is already becoming and becoming is entwined with being. As noted in (2), the simultaneity within the activity of being allows no separation such that being could stand in absolute demarcation from becoming. Perhaps one could say here that being and becoming are always touching, intermingling, and at play with one another in the activity of transformative life, or simply that being is always in a state of becoming. As Nietzsche proclaims, and as a helpful reference to all three of our interventions thus far, "there is no 'being' behind doing, effecting, becoming; 'the doer' is merely a fiction added to the deed – the deed is everything."[13] Here we may have to venture far enough to say that for Nietzsche, being *is* becoming, or that there is no being in itself, only a becoming. In an overly simplified manner we could also here make use of Heidegger's notion of *Dasein*. We can do this, only if we momentarily simplify its meaning as being the movement, differentiation, and spacing implied in the "da" or "there" of there-being.[14] For further insight into the notion of becoming we could also look again to Deleuze's philosophy, in particular Chapter 10 in "A Thousand Plateaus" entitled "1730: Becoming-Intense, Becoming-Animal, Becoming Imperceptible...."

4. There is no point of origin in the sense that each origin erases itself in dissemination.

A continuous movement of "coming to be and becoming other" disavows any sense of origin, for to truly grasp or find an origin, a system of movement must stop or at least be temporarily grounded. For example, if as something is coming to be and at the same time it is becoming something other (to complicate matters even more so, one must realize this is happening as a multiplicity of interstitial occurrences), there is absolutely no

---

[13] Friedrich Nietzsche, *On the Genealogy of Morals and Ecce Homo*, trans. Walter Kaufman and R.J. Hollingdale (New York: Random House, 1967), p. 45.
[14] Here I am referring to Michael Inwood, *A Heidegger Dictionary* (Malden: Blackwell Publishing, 1999), p. 42.

point of reference from which to distinguish a beginning, middle, or end to becoming. In order to have a reference point for such notions as beginning, middle, or end, one must temporarily suspend becoming; therefore one must force it outside the movements of time. As Nietzsche would say, "origin" is a descriptive fiction which allows measure and orientation; it is not a local or fixed point of absolute difference in activity. Here we could begin to look toward Derrida's philosophy of "origin" in language when he states: "'Signifier of the signifier' describes on the contrary the movement of language: in its origin, to be sure, but one can already suspect that an origin whose structure can be expressed as 'signifier of the signifier' conceals and erases itself in its own production."[15]

5. Being and otherness (difference) are inseparable in becoming.

In a state of becoming, otherness or difference is already in being. Pure unity or a totalization of being without difference and thus multiplicity implies an impossible separation from the continuous motion of becoming. In fact, the motion implied in becoming necessitates a continuous relation between being and difference, for the relation in itself is the movement of life. All motion (becoming) in itself is the relation between any attempted unity and difference. Being in becoming is both a type of unity made up of particular attributes gathered together, and a type of difference which is always in excess of the collected unity.[16] Remember, as something "is" it is always also something "other." Being and otherness thus coexist in the continuous unfolding of becoming. Here, it is extremely helpful to make note of the following passage by Derrida where he states: "You see, pure unity or pure multiplicity – when there is only totality or unity and when there is only multiplicity or

---

[15] Jacques Derrida, *Of Grammatology*, trans. Gayatri Spivak (Baltimore: Johns Hopkins University Press, 1976), p. 7.
[16] Here it would be useful to consider Derrida's thinking on this issue when he states that "the relationship of the unity to itself implies some difference." See Jacques Derrida, and John D. Caputo, *Deconstruction in a Nutshell: A Conversation with Jacques Derrida* (New York: Fordham University Press, 1997), p. 13.

disassociation – is a synonym of death."[17] Here, we can now also add the thinking of Jean-Luc Nancy's philosophy of "being singular plural" where once again the emphasis is on both, as compared to one or the other, in the movement of being.

6. All things exist only in relation, even if the relation is as minimal as only to itself.

In "relation," there exists a "between" time and space from which the transformation of being as becoming occurs. The relation is one of similarity and difference – similar in the sense of unity and recognition, and different in the sense of that which is other or differs. Differing is the movement of becoming where in difference to itself or other others it creates a space of between or relation of differentiation from which it unfolds. A multiplicity of relations (in relation) makes up the "milieu" from which otherness as event emerges. Difference as a relation to unity is the catalyst in the movement of becoming, and furthermore, difference as other is that which emerges from the movement or spacing of relation. In short, without relation, or without the "between" of relations, there would be no change or transformation as event. Here, we should look toward Nancy's utilization of Heidegger's notion of *Mitsein*, the "being-with" of being, and Derrida's analysis of unity, difference, and *différance*. I will not go into these notions here, for they are taken up in detail throughout the essay.

7. There is no stable point or fixed moment in being, or there is no "is" in being.

"Is" implies a stability of correlative identity and reducibility to whatever term is placed before or after it. In our analysis, being is irreducible, in the sense that its meaning cannot be reduced to one particular property or another. In fact, it cannot be reduced to even a descriptive multiplicity, for there is always some part which exceeds the descriptive totalization. As mentioned

---

[17] Jacques Derrida, and John D. Caputo, *Deconstruction in a Nutshell: A Conversation with Jacques Derrida* (New York: Fordham University Press, 1997), p. 13.

earlier, in the continuous motion of something becoming another, there is always some point of difference which exceeds the gathering or collection of unity. A pure unity would be reducible to the structure of "is" for it would be fixed and immobile, but the differentiating movement of being in our analysis is unstable and contingent, thus irreducible in meaning. We should perhaps always utilize the "is" within meaning, to really mean "is, but also in excess of."

8.   There is only an excess (more than) of being in transformative becoming.

Becoming is the movement created by the excess or that which exceeds the determination or unity of being. Being is always already in excess of itself in the sense that it is simultaneously of itself and of an-other as difference to itself. Derrida points us to the limit within all attempts at unity or totalization when he says that "the relationship of the unity to itself implies some difference."[18] The limit reached in attempted unity exposes that which exceeds it as difference. In short, there is always some element which slips out, is more than, or is not part of the attempted unity as totalization. The irreducibility and "more than" of being, or the relationship of unity to difference, creates the activity of becoming and event. Throughout this essay, we will periodically utilize Nancy's analysis of the "out of" recognized in the terms "ek" or "ex" in such concepts as ek-stasis (ecstasy), ex-position, etc. What is of interest here is the movement or "thrownness" (Heidegger) implied in the "out of" which comes before certain conceptual configurations. We will also pay particular attention to Derrida's constant analysis of and use of terms which "exceed" any attempts at absolute unity and totalization.

9.   There is a contemporaneous relation between past, present, and future.

---

[18] Derrida speaking at "The Villanova Roundtable" in Jacques Derrida, and John D. Caputo, *Deconstruction in a Nutshell: A Conversation with Jacques Derrida* (New York: Fordham University Press, 1997), p. 13.

Something was, is, and becomes, *at the same time.* There is no determinable point from which to distinguish a pure separation between these pseudo-measures of temporal and spatial becoming. The past exists within the present and the two together within the future. The activity of becoming is *at one time* all three or more or neither. Part-past, part-present, part-future, something becoming becomes. The past, the present, and the future flow into one another in the fluctuating movement of continuous becoming. No absolute line of demarcation separates a pure beginning from an end or a middle point from either of the two. This is not to say that becoming happens outside time or in a temporality of a pure moment. It is simply to say that the past, present, and future intermingle, and that part of each happens or is happening at the same time. Perhaps here again we could look towards the rhizomatic philosophy of Deleuze where he states: "A rhizome has no beginning or end; it is always in the middle, between things, interbeing, *intermezzo.*"[19] It is important to note here that the notion of "middle" for Deleuze is not a localizable fixed point between one thing and another, but the space of and for "transversal movement."[20] Furthermore, it is here that we can begin to glimpse what Derrida means when he speaks in a descriptive manner of a type of aporia which not only exceeds "topographical conditions" but perhaps "the topological condition itself."[21] We will have much to say on the phenomenological conditions of aporias as the essay unfolds, but it can be noted thus far that in a formal sense it can be represented as an open space of possibility and impossibility without any degree of measure. As we will see, the movement or temporary passage (*poros*) out of an aporia is always outside or in excess of the domain of knowledge and certainty; it exists in the "madness" (Kierkegaard) of a decision without measure and predetermined conditions.

---

[19] Gilles Deleuze, and Felix Guattari, *A Thousand Plateaus* (Minneapolis: University of Minnesota Press, 1987), p. 25.

[20] Ibid

[21] Jacques Derrida, *Aporias*, trans. Thomas Dutoit (Stanford: Stanford University Press, 1993), p. 21.

10. There is no future in the sense of "horizon," only a coming in the form of other.

A horizon implies some degree of preconception and thus contains predetermined notions for the coming of that which is hitherto unknown (see Derrida quote below). The becoming other in becoming is always outside the realm of pre-existing knowledge and certainty. If this were not the case, the becoming of something other would simply be more of the same. It is impossible, beforehand, to think the arrival of absolute difference or otherness, for to do so would imply a contradiction in terms. Absolute otherness is by definition that which cannot be thought or expected *a priori*; it always comes as a surprise. As Derrida states: "The *arrivant* must be absolutely other, the other I expect not to be expecting, that I'm not waiting for, whose expectation is made of a nonexpectation, an expectation without what in philosophy is called a horizon of expectation, when a certain knowledge still anticipates and amortizes in advance. If I am sure that there is going to be an event, this will not be an event."[22]   We see that it is only in the realm of uncertain and unforeseen conditions that an other as absolutely other can emerge. The phrase "as something is coming to be it is always already becoming something other" leaves open the indeterminable space for the to-come of the future, for otherness is always already implied in the movement of becoming. Otherness and difference thus serve a double function; on one hand they exceed and thus create the open space outside attempted unity, and on the other hand they arrive unanticipated, unexpected, and undetermined, in the to-come of becoming and event.

1.3 An Undercurrent to Aporetic Openings: Reverberations of Continuous Becoming

[22] Jacques Derrida, and Bernard Stiegler, *Echographies of Television*, trans. Jennifer Bajorek (Cambridge: Polity Blackwell, 2002), p. 13.

We must now briefly sketch out the ontological, phenomenological, epistemological, psychological, ethical, and political implications of the ten interventions listed above. Each of these sketches will serve as an undercurrent to our thinking on aporetic openings. As a preliminary note, I wish to point out from the beginning that I do not believe it useful to think of these "domains" as *separate* entities within philosophical thought or thinking.[23] In fact, I believe the phrase we are now in the process of analyzing disrupts any possibility of absolutely separating each domain from that of the others. Each "domain" contains elements which when considered or reconsidered in relation to our beginning phrase, have an effect on the others. In short, each domain here will be considered separately, but keep in mind the influence each domain has upon the others. There simply is no productive way to think "as something is coming to be it is always already becoming something other" without taking into consideration not only each domain listed, but how each one blends into and with the others. Remember, each domain thought out in relation to our phrase also serves as an introductory precursor to how these domains are utilized throughout the essay at hand.

In summarization:

Ontology – The ontology affirmed here is one of continuous movement, spacing, and transformation. It is an ontology of being *as* becoming. Being is always already in relation to an other, thus being is also always "being-with" (Heidegger, Nancy). There is no stable ground for being in the sense that being as becoming is always over "there" (*Da-sein*), always in differentiation, and always in excess of itself. It is an ontology recognized as transient being. One cannot grasp *being in itself,*

---

[23] I find it much more interesting to think of philosophy along the lines of that espoused by Alain Badiou. Badiou places philosophy within the realm of four conditions: science, love, art, and politics. These conditions are "truth procedures," they "produce truths," and philosophy works in relation to these conditions. This relation is complex and here is not the time or place for an analysis of how philosophy interacts with the conditions. For a thorough understanding of this see the text by Alain Badiou, *Manifesto for Philosophy*, trans. Norman Madarasz (Albany: State University of New York Press, 1999).

for being *as* becoming is always already more than or something other than the attempted identity or unity. Being escapes any determination and absolute ground for conceptualization. Being as becoming is thus uncertain – not a grounded notion of uncertainty in binary opposition to certainty, but an uncertainty marked by a limit in unity, and furthermore an uncertainty exposed in the opening of the absolute other as difference to-come. It will also be suggested in section 2.4 that Derrida's notion of *différance* performs an activity analogous to the ontological considerations thus mentioned. Is the becoming of being a movement analogous to *différance*? We will investigate this question.

Phenomenology – In a state of becoming, there is a coeval movement of concealment and unconcealment (Heidegger). As some-thing becomes it reveals its partial newness and simultaneously conceals not only part of what it once was, but also what it may become. In continuous transformation, some-thing (concept, subject, object, etc.) comes that was not hitherto shown, and something goes that was once recognized in the temporary unity of identity and identification. As Sylviane Agacinski succinctly states, "Like change, time always *makes* and *unmakes* 'at the same time.'"[24] The making and unmaking of continuous becoming simultaneously opens the space for disclosing that which may come, and closes off into the realm of memory that which was known. We are thus left with the illusive memory of what was, the transience of what is, and the possibility of what may become. Once again, and this time in a phenomenological sense, uncertainty prevails. We will look closely at the idea of affirming an "aporetic phenomenology" which in its simultaneous opening/closing accentuates the notion of possibility within impossibility.

Epistemology – As mentioned and affirmed, all things (concepts, words, objects, subjects, etc.) are in a state of becoming. Gaining knowledge or insight into any of these particulars thus entails an unstable terrain. If some-thing is constantly in a state

---

[24] Sylviane Agacinski, *Time Passing*, European Perspectives, trans. Jody Gladding (New York: Columbia University Press, 2003), p. 16.

of also becoming some-thing other, there is no stable ground for absolute knowledge and judgment. Furthermore, and to complicate matters even more so, it is not only the object being considered that exists in a state of transformation, but also the "subject" doing the interpretation. What we have left is a thoroughly perspectival (Nietzsche) relation to viewing and interpreting what we see and know of this world. By affirming this, knowledge becomes not a ground or an end in itself, but the means for a continual perspectival shifting. Perspectivism, as a thoroughly ungrounded and continuously shifting mode of interpretation, furthermore affirms the uncertainty of an indeterminate subject, object, and conceptual becoming.

Psychology – Perhaps more important here is an understanding of mood or *Stimmung* (Heidegger). The uncertainty of transformative becoming adheres to a fundamental sense of *Angst* or anxiety. In the "between" space of the becoming of being, a zone of indeterminacy prevails – a spacing which is in accordance with ontological anxiety. We are not only thrown (Heidegger) into this world, but more so continuously thrown outside ourselves or in excess of our being by the movements of becoming. As Heidegger would say, we are always in the movement toward (*zu*) - toward-being, toward-others, toward-death, etc. Indeterminate becoming furthermore exposes us to the pure opening of nothing or the open space of possibility and uncertainty. For Heidegger and Kierkegaard, anxiety is that which occurs in relation to nothing, or no identifiable thing in itself. Anxiety occurs in the open space of an opening (Nancy) without measure and identification. Aporias thus have an intimate two-fold relation to anxiety, in the sense that aporias not only create anxiety, but anxiety furthermore maintains the open aporetic space of possibility/impossibility. An uncritical passage (*poros*) of determined pseudo-certitude simply closes down anxiety and the ethical possibility of making a decision within the realm of indecision. Of essential importance therefore is an affirmation of staying with and enduring the anxiety of becoming. Kierkegaard perhaps summarizes all of this when he states, "anxiety is freedom's actuality as the possibility of possibility."[25]

Ethics – The ethical stance here, therefore, is not one of foundation or determinacy. It is a stance situated in a contextual realm where continuous creation and invention replaces that of an uncritical mechanistic and dogmatic application. A thoroughly transformative world of becoming calls for an ethics exposed and open to the not-yet-known or to-come of the future. It is an ethics created within the impossibility of a stable ground for determination, and an ethics open to the indeterminacy of incessant becoming. In emphasis of this point, and furthermore bridging both domains of psychology and ethics, Miguel de Unamuno states, "What I wish to establish is that uncertainty, doubt, perpetual wrestling with the mystery of our final destiny, mental despair, and the lack of any solid and stable dogmatic foundation, may be the basis of an ethic."[26] This existential stance is of importance for it combines the uncertainty, the anxiety, and the instability of transformative becoming into a possible precursor to thinking ethics. An ethical stance, as such, could only be inventive and furthermore always open to its own ongoing transformation. This existential sensibility (mood, *Stimmung*) affirms the idea that ethics can never be grounded in certainty for certitude in totalization closes the open transformative space for becoming or that which is yet to come. Here, we will look toward Derrida's philosophy which emphasizes an aporetic ethics, or an ethics situated in the possibility within impossibility, and an ethics which is always to come. We will also look toward Wolfgang Schirmacher's notion of an ethics which occurs in an "imperceptible" manner – a manner which is intimately tied to fulfillment in a generating/inventive movement of becoming.

Politics – Connected to the ethical stance above, the type of politics suited for a philosophy of becoming is a politics structured around the impossibility of totalization or completion.

---

[25] Soren Kierkegaard, *The Concept of Anxiety*, trans. Reider Thomte (Princeton: Princeton University Press, 1980), p. 42.

[26] Miguel de Unamuno, *Tragic Sense of Life*, trans. J. E. Crawford Flitch (New York: Barnes and Noble Publishing, 1913, c2006), p. 230.

The type of politics thus affirmed here is one of democracy. Here we must make use however of Derrida's notion of "democracy-to-come" – a democracy understood in the sense that it never absolutely "arrive at plenitude or come to presence."[27] In short, a democracy as such should never absolutely arrive or fulfill itself in absolute unity, for this would paradoxically fold into a totalized (totalitarian) and completed structure of political design. By definition, democracy cannot complete itself; it must stay open to an indeterminate future to come. We could state here in correlation with our beginning quote that as democracy is and is coming to be, it should always be open to becoming, or to the other as difference to come. Democracy must stay open (even in difficult times) to the uncertain and undecidable space for becoming, otherwise it risks the closure of totalization. Democracy must endure the aporia of being possible only in relation to an impossible completion.

1.4 Aporetic Openings: Spacing, Differentiation, and the To-Come of Becoming

> I will even venture to say that ethics, politics, and responsibility, *if there are any*, will only ever have begun with the experience and experiment of the aporia.[28]
>
> - Jacques Derrida

The experiment and experience of the aporia is thus the emphasis of the essay at hand. To think within the uncertain terrain of aporias allows thinking to remain in an ungrounded and indeterminate space for the to-come of continuous becoming. Uncertainty within this "undecidable" (Derrida) and aporetic space does not lead to infinite deferral or indefinite suspension as some may suspect. On the contrary, and here following the logic of Derrida, it provides nothing other than the

---

[27] Niall Lucy, *A Derrida Dictionary* (Malden: Blackwell Publishing, 2004), p. 18.

[28] Jacques Derrida, *The Other Heading*, trans. Pascale-Anne Brault and Michael B. Naas (Bloomington: Indiana University Press, 1992), p. 41.

possibility for a true decision to occur. The experience of an aporia allows a true decision to emerge – a decision without measure and without predetermined criteria. A decision is thus made in the uncertainty of indecision. It is furthermore the ceaseless movement of uncertainty within an aporia which allows a continuous becoming, a spacing, a differentiation, and an always already other to emerge. The ambiguous non-passage of an aporia is thus not a lack or deficiency, but a potentiality and possibility within the fabric of an event to come. The movement of becoming is a movement of differentiation, a differentiating which produces openings for "sense,"[29] new meanings, novelty, and event. These temporal and spatial openings are produced by the restless movement of becoming which is always open to the otherness of which it may become. The always other of becoming through differentiation is created by and creates in one gesture the anxiety of being - an ontological anxiety which allows thought to remain within the realm of uncertainty and thus in the ambiguous space of an ethical decision. The decision marks the temporary passage (*poros*) out of the aporia, but it soon thereafter must open itself once again to the uncertain space for new and other decisions to come. Aporias allow temporary passage (*poros*), but they remain forever open in the indeterminate space for the becoming of that which is yet to come, whether in the realm of (inventive) ethics, politics, or the becoming of being.

---

[29] Throughout the essay, I will constantly make use of Jean-Luc Nancy's notion of "sense." This term will become clear as the essay unfolds.

Part 2: An Aporetic and Undecidable Philosophy to Come: Jacques Derrida

2.1 Aporias: Possibility within Impossibility

> The condition of possibility of this thing called responsibility is a certain *experience and experiment of the possibility of the impossible: the testing of the aporia* from which one may invent the only *possible invention, the impossible invention.*[30]
>
> - Jacques Derrida

The concept of responsibility, for Derrida, is intimately entwined with other notions such as duty, decision, ethics, and politics. The term "responsibility" therefore functions in a trans-literal fashion, moving about throughout his thinking, here and there finding its way into varying configurations of ethical and political importance. What is also always around, near, or in close proximity to these conceptual configurations is the notion of aporia. This complex and antinomic term (aporia) more than any other, continuously shadows any thinking on ethics, politics, etc., which attempts to "find its way" (*poros*) in any steadfast, clear, or determinable fashion. With this in mind, we must attempt a close analysis of the term aporia in an attempt to open up its various potentialities for ethical and political thinking. But here, we must also maintain a somewhat cautious approach to this term, for in many ways it tends to evade absolute sense, binary logic, and foundational meaning. We will thus approach the term from various angles of intervention. This strategy will perhaps not only allow us a glimpse into the potentiality of the term, but also the spatial and temporal configurations for thinking as such. In short, what does an aporia give, allow, or open up for thinking, and furthermore, what would it entail to be

---

[30] Jacques Derrida, *The Other Heading*, trans. Pascale-Anne Brault and Michael B. Naas (Bloomington: Indiana University Press, 1992), p. 41.

caught up in thinking aporetically? These questions may help us in understanding what Derrida means by an "experience," "experiment," or "testing of the aporia" as mentioned in the above quote. But again, and as a note of precaution, this will not be an easy task, for as Derrida asks in another text: "Can one speak – and if so, in what sense – of *an experience of the aporia*? An experience *of the aporia as such*? Or vice versa: Is an experience possible that would not be an experience of the aporia?"[31]

We can sense already the complexity involved in speaking of an experience of the aporia. On one hand, we may be attempting to speak of an aporetic experience in retrospect, and on another hand, we may be attempting to communicate an aporetic experience from within the experience itself. The paradox of the latter case is that in life we never stop experiencing. We cannot shut off experience, thus if experience is aporetic as such, we may be attempting to speak of aporias from within aporias. Furthermore, how can we communicate a particular sense of experience from within the confines of that particular experience itself?[32] Don't we always need a reference of other or some topography from which to communicate, discuss, or explain? And outside these antinomies, what is "experience" in itself, with or without aporias? The questions here may continue to unfold in a labyrinthine manner, so perhaps now we should slow down our questioning, continue on with a slow sense of caution, and begin first and foremost with an analysis of the term "aporia" in and of itself.

A literal translation of aporia is from the Greek *aporos* which means "without passage" or impassable. In various ways outside the literal meaning, the term usually revolves around

---

[31] Jacques Derrida, *Aporias*, trans. Thomas Dutoit (Stanford: Stanford University Press, 1993), p. 15.

[32] Now is not the place, but an interesting point of departure into this line of questioning would be to start with an analysis of John Dewey's philosophy of experience. For Dewey, experience always takes place in the interplay between such notions as stability and instability. Furthermore, we have an experience *of* this interplay and experience existence *in* this interplay. Experience occurs on both levels – both in and of what Dewey calls nature. For more on this, see page xxv in *The Philosophy of John Dewey*, ed. John J. McDermott (Chicago: University of Chicago Press). McDermott discusses this in the Introduction.

such notions as "an irresolvable internal contradiction," "an expression of uncertainty or doubt as to how to proceed," "to be at a loss," or at times just simply a "difficult passage."[33] The list of definitions goes on, but the important thing to notice is the varying degrees of intensity from no passage to difficult passage, and all the accompanying degrees of uncertainty and doubt. When it comes to the other of aporia, we get the term *poros*, which literally means "passage." From *poros* we of course get the word pore or pores from which we can understand the passage that occurs from the inside to the outside of the body and vice versa. In this sense we usually come to think of passage as that which promotes circulation, movement, and a type of bodily breathing which exists in correlation with the health of a living organism. We also tend to favor the idea that the mind should function according to principles of passage. To be uncertain, in doubt, to be perplexed, in hesitation, or in the restlessness (Nancy) of indecision is usually considered a state from which one should quickly depart by way of resolve. In many ways being at an impasse is usually considered a temporary space from which one should flee as soon as possible. Being caught up in the anxiety of indecision is usually thought of as a sign of indeterminate being, and thus viewed as a weakness of mind. We are usually taught already as children to not only decide in a determined manner, but to think and thus decide as quickly as possible. The problem here is not so much the step away from indecision, (although as I will later suggest is done too quickly) but the consequences of holding on to that decision in a closed and definitive manner. In other words, a decision is necessary but only to such a degree that it remains exposed to the possibility of becoming something other. In short, it must not attempt an absolute unity or identity which leads to a fundamental closure. A decision should also recognize its own limit of being possible only within or in relation to impossibility and impossible completion. What does this mean? It suggests that in relation to responsibility, one must always make a decision, but the decision in itself, by way of its singular passage, also closes off all the other possibilities. The

---

[33] These definitions were all found by searching through various online dictionaries at http://onelook.com

impossibility lies in not being able to fulfill, by way of decision, each and every possible space or being that calls one toward the act of decision. There is always something left outside, left unanswered, or unheard in the act of every decision. This impossibility should not point to absolute indecision or suspension, but more so to the responsibility of deciding in the face of this impossibility. It opens us to the leap or madness (Kierkegaard) implied in every decision. Every decision originates in the space of indecision, and as responsibility, its possibility exists within impossibility. This configuration points us already to the *poros* implied within the space of *aporos*.

The situation therefore is not whether one should favor the indeterminacy of *aporos* over the determinacy of *poros*, or vice versa, but to see these terms as coexisting and at play within one another. It is essential to no longer view these concepts in binary opposition but begin to see them as concepts which continuously fold over and into one another. In fact, the folding interplay (a non-dialectical movement) from one within the other gives each of them their own possibility of periodic and independent expression. We could perhaps suggest here that *aporos* and *poros* coexist in a Heideggerian, revealing and concealing, phenomenology. The showing of one does not simply cancel the other out; it more so allows a *degree* of expression to become manifest. Again, we should attempt to think outside the either/or of binary opposition in regard to these terms, and instead think in terms of a transformative both. They happen together – they coexist in joint movements, in a simultaneous occurrence where one gives life to that of the other. *Aporos* and *poros* need one another in a continuous interactivity of play, for one without the other, in totalized separation from the other, leads to the metaphysics implied in absolute determinacy and absolute indeterminacy. To demand decision over indecision, determinacy over indeterminacy, unity over difference, etc., thus entirely misses the point. *Poros* without *aporos* leads to totalized closure, and *aporos* without *poros* leads to pure suspension. Their interplay creates the possible in relation to the impossible. How they coexist and in what manner they intermingle, we shall now explore.

In "Beyond Aporia?," Sarah Kofman warns us again of the difficulty in translating the terms *poros* and *aporos*. She understands that both terms break with "the logic of identity"[34] implied in an attempt at locating a particular meaning within one word or the other. Each word in and of itself exceeds the attempted unity necessary for translated and individualized identity. Basically, the meaning of each term flows over and beyond any totalized unity implied in separate identification. So, where does this lead us in regard to understanding these terms? We must look into the ways in which each word has an effect on the other. Perhaps looking at the terms *poros* and *aporos* as inseparable notions, we can gain insight into their respective differences as compared to their so called separate identities. Most importantly, we should look for what each word does, how each word acts on its own and in relation to the other, how each word moves and interacts, and how each creates its own sense of space and time. What does *poros* create and how does it make its way? How fast or how slow, and in what way does it create its passage? What is the space of aporetic indeterminacy? Does the determinacy of *poros* move in a time in differentiation to the uncertainty of *aporos*, or do they create a temporal and spatial sensibility together? In short, what activity is implied in each of these terms?

Of central importance, Kofman immediately points us to the difference implied in the seemingly similar terms *odos* and *poros*. *Odos* is "a path or a road of any kind," whereas *poros* refers "to a sea-route or a route down the river."[35] The initial difference here shows itself to us by way of metaphor. *Odos*, as road or path, is created and paved on the stable ground of earth, while *poros* makes its way, its passage, through the instability of the moving waters. *Odos* paves its way on stable ground while *poros* makes its passage in the midst of the chaotic and unknown movements of the river or sea. As we can sense, *poros* makes a route or direction from within the ungrounded movement of continuous change. In this sense, *poros* creates a sense of

---

[34] Sarah Kofman, "Beyond Aporia?," in *Post-Structuralist Classics*, ed. Andrew Benjamin (New York: Routledge, 1988), p. 10.
[35] Sarah Kofman, "Beyond Aporia?," in *Post-Structuralist Classics*, ed. Andrew Benjamin (New York: Routledge, 1988), p. 10.

temporary stability out of the context of instability, a sense of temporary order in the midst of disorder. Notice that *poros* does not make its way by means of previous paths, marks, or signs; it creates its own way in a space "initially devoid of all contours."[36] This is why Kofman states: "To say that *poros* is a way to be found across an expanse of liquid is to stress that a *poros* is never traced in advance, that it can always be obliterated, that it must always be traced anew, in unprecedented fashion."[37]   *Poros* makes a way, creates a passage, but the passage in itself is always subject to the turbulence from which it was created. If a passage disappears, the future passages to come will not be able to rely on those that preceded it; each passage must each and every time be created anew. Furthermore, the passage cannot be "traced in advance" for the context is always already shifting. As Derrida would say in regard to how and where to begin, we must simply "start wherever we are."

We see here already three essential points:

1.   The possibility of *poros*, passage, and thus determinacy comes from a space of indeterminacy.
2.   There is a continuous interplay between *poros* and indeterminacy.
3.   The passage (*poros*) created within a space of indeterminacy is only momentarily fixed and stable, for it is always exposed to turbulence from which it arose.

Holding on to these three points, we will move now to a quote by Kofman which brings together in summation the intimate relation between *poros* and what we will now call *aporos*. She states:

> One speaks of a *poros* when it is a matter of blazing a trail where no trail exists, of crossing an impassable expanse of territory, an unknown,

---

[36] Ibid
[37] Ibid

hostile and boundless world, an *apeiron* which it
is impossible to cross from end to end; ....[38]

We see here once again, that *poros* makes its way, defines its
path, and creates its passage, initially in a space *without passage*
(aporia). *Poros* creates the lines, the dimensions, and the time
necessary for passage through the boundless space of *apeiron*.
This is the creative and inventive form of *poros* (decision) which
"blazes a trail" where no trail hitherto has existed or exists.
Each time anew *poros* creates its own possibility within the
impossible terrain of boundless and indeterminate *apeiron*.
Making decisions here, in this space of contextual
indeterminacy, is truly to make a decision, for the decision did
not come by means of predetermined conditions; it was
inventive through and through. To make a decision in such a
terrain is to decide without the necessities of absolute certainty
or absolute knowledge. It is to expose oneself to creative
becoming – a continuous movement of being which creates
passage (*poros*) in the never ending shift of contextual
configurations. Here perhaps we could make use of Wolfgang
Schirmacher's notion of "homo generator," which
simultaneously calls attention to the becoming, inventing, and
creating nature of being in the world. Homo generator is "a
human being that needs no Being, no certainty, no truth."[39] As
such, this human being makes decisions not based simply on
what was, but what is now, and what is to come. Homo
generator thinks within the shifting context, and each time in the
act of making a decision, he or she creates a context of his/her
own. At play in the movement of continuous becoming, homo
generator affirms the generating and inventive movement
through life. This being affirms the interplay of *poros* and
aporos, the movement of decision made without the certainty of
completion and absolute truth. Homo generator generates and
continues to generate each time anew. It does so in the interplay
of *poros* and *aporos*.

---

[38] Ibid
[39] Wolfgang Schirmacher, "Homo Generator: Media and Postmodern
Technology," in *Culture on the Brink*, ed. Gretchen Bender and Timothy
Druckrey (Seattle: Bay Press, 1994), p. 70.

We need not venture further in our analysis to see that *poros* and *aporos* coexist in an interactive relationship where one does not simply erase the other. The interplay that exists between them is the space from which such notions as a decision within indecision or determinacy within indeterminacy arise. For Derrida, the moment of decision is always surrounded by a context of indecision. Furthermore, a decision made as such – a decision made in the tumultuous space of aporia must also always finds its way anew. Any decision which does not simultaneously open itself up to other possibilities risks the danger of becoming totalized and absolute. A decision must be made in an aporia, but the decision must also not fall into a totalized path of identity or unity. In short, a decision must on one hand make its passage out of the aporia, but on another hand it should never find its home in absolute certitude outside the aporetic terrain. Here we could perhaps make use of Alain Badiou's notion of fidelity as compared to that of certitude in decision. With fidelity there is commitment and perhaps a type of surety, but never the kind which closes off the possibility for future events to come. For Badiou, each truth must in some form or another leave itself open to the possibility of becoming something other. Without this open and "unnameable" part in any truth process, the truth simply becomes a totalized and therefore dogmatic principle. Fidelity to a particular event of truth does not entail an uncritical following or dogmatic desire; it more so signifies a decision structured around an incessant void of affirmed incompletion. If an event of truth fills itself, or closes itself only with itself, it becomes in Badiou's words a "simulacrum of truth."[40] This of course is an extremely dangerous truth event, for it seeks only to fill its void with a totalized and complete meaning of itself. In other words, it tries to fulfill itself in the closure of its own absolute identity. In regard to ethics, this closed identity merely becomes the likes of an intolerant and fundamental morality, and in political terms, a totalitarian regime. A "truth process" (Badiou) must never absolutely fulfill itself with its own identity or unity as one; it must always be open to the transformation implied in the

---

[40] Alain Badiou, *Ethics*, trans. Peter Hallward (London: Verso, 2001), p. 73.

ongoing relationship of multiplicities. For Badiou, a decision cuts through the fabric or backdrop of a world made up of "indifferent multiplicities."[41] Unity, or a collected multiplicity, is understood only as a temporary mode held together in the decision – a "counting as one."[42] This "count" is not a stable, fixed, or closed mode, but a decision made within the realm of multiple multiplicities. A decision holds together, as a singular decision, a temporary and open collected unity in the face of the absolute indeterminacy of pure multiplicity. It would be tempting here to analogously align the indeterminacy of "indifferent multiplicities" with the indeterminacy of *aporos* and *apeiron*. In both cases, a decision as *poros* emerges from within, or we could say, in the face of an uncertain and boundless space without measure. It seems, in this regard, Badiou and Derrida may not be as far apart in their philosophies as many would have it.

In the chapters that follow, we will see how Derrida makes use of the notion of aporia we have here exposed. We can simply say at this point and in summation, that as *poros* is in play with *aporos*, decision is in play with indecision, determinacy in play with indeterminacy, certainty with uncertainty, and most importantly, possibility is at all times interwoven into the texture of impossibility. This is the aporetic space from which Derrida in various ways discusses the ethical and political possibilities of our time. One within the other, *poros* with *aporos*, an interplay not of either/or, but of a simultaneous gesture of both.

2.2 A Future To-Come: (*l'venir, a venir*)

> Opening oneself to what comes can be a way of
> exposing oneself to the future [*a l'avenir*] or to

---

[41] Alain Badiou, *Being and Event*, trans. Oliver Feltham (London: Continuum, 2005).
[42] Ibid

the coming of the other, to the coming that does
not depend on me.[43]

- Jacques Derrida

As soon as you address the other, as soon as you
are open to the future, as soon as you have a
temporal experience of waiting for the future, of
waiting for someone to come: that is the opening
of experience. Someone is to come, is *now* to
come.[44]

- Jacques Derrida

It is on condition of this "come" that there is an
experience of coming, of the event, of what is
happening, and consequently, of that which,
because it comes from the other, cannot be
anticipated.[45]

- Jacques Derrida

We spend a vast amount of time and energy attempting to
determine an indeterminable future. Day by day, we plan and
order our existence in such a way that we *hope* each determined
action or thought leads to a reciprocated determined outcome.
This attempt or strategy for life in the face of an impossible
certainty could perhaps be understood as the courage for
existence itself.[46] It is part and parcel of an attempt at dealing
with the essential finitude of human existence. We live, in other
words, in a constant reminder of our limits, our inability to
forecast and absolutely determine our projected future. And yet,

---

[43] Jacques Derrida, and Maurizio Ferraris, *A Taste for the Secret*, trans. Giacomo
Donis (Malden: Polity Blackwell Publishers, 2001), p. 60.
[44] Jacques Derrida, and John D. Caputo, *Deconstruction in a Nutshell: A
Conversation with Jacques Derrida* (New York: Fordham University Press,
1997), p. 22.
[45] Jacques Derrida, and Bernard Stiegler, *Echographies of Television*, trans.
Jennifer Bajorek (Cambridge: Polity Press, 2002), p. 12.
[46] Here one could look at various "existential" texts, but for particular insight into
this thinking see perhaps Paul Tillich, *The Courage to Be* (New Haven: Yale
University Press, 1952).

we continue to press ahead with our planning, *as if*, we were not staring directly into a future of incessant indeterminacy. In fact, perhaps we plan with such determinacy, to spite indeterminacy itself. This is one way, and here I would say, an "existential" way of dealing with the absolute finite nature of existence. But let's look closer. Let's look at the structure of thinking along with the projecting of a determinate future in the midst of indeterminacy. In other words, what is occurring in the aporia of finite being, or, in the space where determinacy is at odds with an indeterminate future?

Near the end of *Siddhartha*, the short novel by Herman Hesse, Siddhartha realizes that many of the projected goals he set for himself in life simply led him nowhere. In fact, he realizes that the determined ideas (in regard to what he should be or become), in and of themselves, destroyed his actual ability *to become*. Here I will quote for emphasis.

> When someone is seeking, said Siddhartha, it happens quite easily that he only sees the thing that he is seeking; that he is unable to find anything, unable to absorb anything, because he is only thinking of the thing he is seeking, because he has a goal, because he is obsessed with his goal. Seeking means: to have a goal; but finding means: to be free, to be receptive, to have no goal.[47]

As we can see, for Siddhartha, seeking or projecting into the future leads paradoxically to "finding" nothing. What one "finds" when one seeks is only that entity which one sought, therefore nothing was ever truly found. Finding, in the truest sense of the word, is related to the receptivity of coming, or as Derrida would say, the absolute other. In other words, seeking is a projection into the future of an anticipated and thus determined arrival, whereas finding, or the "to find" of existence, is open to the indeterminacy of what may or may not come. Being open to the indeterminacy of "to come" allows for a "finding" in the

---

[47] Hermann Hesse, *Siddhartha*, trans. Hilda Rosner (New York: New Directions, 1951), p. 140.

truest sense of the word, for "to find" is always only in relation to the unexpected. This is why Derrida says that the event, the coming of the other as other "cannot be anticipated." If we anticipate, expect, or have a predetermined understanding of what is coming, nothing will truly come as other. The other is only other (as difference in itself) by coming from an elsewhere outside the realm of "seeking," or from a predetermined condition of arrival. The event, or coming of the other, can only arrive without determinacy and expectation. As Derrida says (and here he is referring to a "messianicity before messianism"[48]), "If there were a horizon of expectation, if there were anticipation or programming, there would be neither event nor history."[49] This of course is not a suggestion by Derrida that one should abandon all such notions as projecting, planning, determining, etc., but more so an attempt to highlight the importance of the incalculable, especially when it comes to such notions as responsibility, hospitality, and justice. These terms, for Derrida, are possible only in relation to the impossibility of absolute determinability. In short, each of them are possible only within an indeterminate and thus always open "to come" of the future. To determine or have conditions for who may or may not come is certainly not hospitality, for according to Derrida, "absolute hospitality" requires an "absolute *arrivant*,"[50] or, the possibility for an absolute other to come. Again, the arrival of the other as other must by definition exceed any so called conditions, preconditions, or predetermined knowledge. As with justice and responsibility, they must all exceed any determinable configuration. Following the rules or a recognized path in life may be good, moral, and in accordance with the law, but it is not, according to Derrida, justice or responsibility. All three of these terms, hospitality, responsibility, and justice, exist only in the aporetic space of being possible and impossible at the same time. They are possible only because they exceed the realm of

---

[48] Derrida uses this phrase to emphasize a notion of coming which precedes any understanding of coming whatsoever. He is attempting to describe perhaps the condition of and for coming. The phrase "messianicity before messianism" also points to a notion of "to-come" without the religious connotations.

[49] Jacques Derrida, and Bernard Stiegler, *Echographies of Television*, trans. Jennifer Bajorek (Cambridge: Polity Press, 2002), p. 12.

[50] Ibid

hitherto pre-thought or predetermined conditions. It is only within the "to come" of the future that they may or may not arrive. The possibility for arrival consists of the impossibility of determination.

We can thus recognize that there are other (somewhat known and yet unknown) alternative routes in dealing with an indefinite and uncertain future. The finitude of being and becoming may provoke a determinacy in existence, but it may also allow a sensibility open to event, or the coming of absolute difference. Again, it need not be one way or the other, for there is value at times in both ways of approaching an uncertain future. What is perhaps certain here is that too much determinacy, too much decision making in the guise of certitude, and too much acceptance of only that which is predetermined and thus part of the same, leads to a closing down of any form of event. This type of absolute determinate thinking shuts down the "to come" of the future, and as Derrida says, "the opening of experience."

2.3 Excess of/and Elsewhere

> What disrupts the totality is the condition for the relation to the other. The privilege granted to unity, to totality, to organic ensembles, to community as a homogenized whole – this is a danger for responsibility, for decision, for ethics, for politics.[51]
>
> - Jacques Derrida

> What interests me is the limit of every attempt to totalize, to gather, *versammeln*... - the limit of this unifying, uniting movement, the limit that it

---

[51] This is Derrida speaking at a Villanova roundtable discussion on Oct. 2, 1994. It was published in: Jacques Derrida, and John D. Caputo, *Deconstruction in a Nutshell: A Conversation with Jacques Derrida* (New York: Fordham University Press, 1997), p. 13.

had to encounter, because the relationship of the
unity to itself implies some difference.[52]

- Jacques Derrida

In *What is Called Thinking?* (*Was Heisst Denken?*),
Heidegger, in a lengthy, poetic and yet rigorous fashion,
analyzes the nature of thinking and thought. He points us to the
ambiguity and play of meaning in the verb "*heissen,*" which may
be understood as "to name" or more importantly for his analysis
on thinking, to function as "to call." In the former sense (to
name), *Was Heisst Denken?* carries a meaning such as, what
does thinking mean, or, what does the word "thinking" signify?,
and in the latter sense (to call), the question asks, what is it that
calls us into thinking? Here is not the place for a thorough
analysis of Heidegger's thinking on this, but it should be noted
that for Heidegger, thinking happens along the lines of being
called *toward,* or invited *toward* thought. Thinking is not a
projection of what one already knows, but an openness opened
by the call of thought toward thinking. Being called and drawn
toward that which withdraws is for Heidegger the path toward
thinking. Heidegger states:

> Once we are so related and drawn to that which
> withdraws, we are drawing into what withdraws,
> into the enigmatic and therefore mutable
> nearness of its appeal. Whenever man is
> properly drawing that way, he is thinking – even
> though he may still be far away from what
> withdraws, even though the withdrawal may
> remain as veiled as ever.[53]

For Heidegger, to be thinking is to be underway (*unterweg*), to
be caught in the current of that thought or question which calls
us toward it without the desire or quest for knowledge in the
form of an answer. This is why Heidegger also says "that in the

---

[52] Ibid
[53] Martin Heidegger, *What is Called Thinking?* (New York: Harper & Row, 1972, c1968), p. 17.

widest sense, 'to call' means to set in motion."[54] A question thus appeals to the movement of thought, as compared to an absolute answer which merely shuts down the space left open for further thinking. In this sense, the question thus functions as the precursor to such notions as contingency, possibility, and uncertainty, for the question calls thinking away from the immobile stability of ground and absolute certainty. In fact, this type of thinking pulls thought away from attempted unity and opens it up to the movement implied in difference and alterity. Here, of course, (and we will get to this later) Heidegger and Derrida, to a certain degree in their thinking, part ways.

A question here will thus keep our thinking in motion – a movement toward thinking on and around the various configurations of responsibility, totality, and how the relationship of unity to itself implies difference, as stated in the opening quotes to this section by Derrida. In other words, we must begin to think toward that which possibly exceeds or escapes unity and totalization. Again it will be a question. Our question will not call us toward an answer or a passage (*poros*) through to a particular point, but toward thinking in an open aporetic space of uncertainty, indeterminacy, and undecidability. It is within this anxious, ambiguous, and enigmatic (to refer back to Heidegger's quote) space of aporia that our thinking will be open not to what we already know, but to perhaps what is yet to come. It is the time in front of us, the time which is coming, which gives us the possibility of thinking something other, some-thing, a thought or thoughts, suspended in the temporality of the not yet (Derrida).   Thought reaches us, touches us perhaps, as Jean-Luc Nancy would say, on the border and limit of the here and now, but thought comes or is always coming to us from somewhere else temporally and spatially beyond. In short, thought comes to us from "elsewhere." Elsewhere draws us to the border of thought, to the finitude of our being, and to the limit of our knowledge at each and every moment, but it also allows (by the incessant coming of that which hitherto was unknown), a constant shifting of limits, borders, and horizons. Elsewhere is the source of novelty and event. Elsewhere gives,

---

[54] Heidegger, *What is Called Thinking?*, p. 117.

as in the Heideggerian notion of "*es gibt*," yet simultaneously, it draws us into its withdrawal. Without elsewhere, we only have a here, a there, a present moment and the past. With an elsewhere we have a future to come. We also therefore have the continuous withdrawal into the enigma of that which is not yet known, and thus with an elsewhere we have the potentiality toward thinking as understood by Heidegger.

So, we must now pose the question which will continue our thinking on and in proximity to Derrida's earlier quotes. This question will hopefully move us toward a better understanding of those opening lines. It is a question in relation to the notion of "elsewhere." Quite simply, where is elsewhere, and in particular, how are we to think not only the elsewhere of Derrida, but the elsewhere that Derrida has given us to think? Again, let's not look for the passage (*poros*) of an answer or answers, but for where this question of *where* takes us. Here, we can start by listening to Derrida himself. I quote here from the opening lines of the documentary film entitled "Derrida's Elsewhere" by Safaa Fathy.

> I have long thought that the name of writing, of deconstruction, of phallogocentrism, etc., must stem from this strange reference to an elsewhere. Childhood, the other side of the Mediterranean, French culture, Europe… It means thought springing from the moment you cross a frontier. Elsewhere, even when nearby, is always beyond a certain limit.[55]

As seen, we can get close to elsewhere, or as Derrida says, it can be nearby. We can perhaps get infinitesimally close to the limit, or border, yet elsewhere is always "beyond a certain limit." Perhaps, as Jean-Luc Nancy would say, we can touch the border, but penetration over into elsewhere is an intrusion. To reach elsewhere would entail the violence of totalization, the absolute closure of the excess of being and thought which gives us the "to

---

[55] "Derrida's Elsewhere," transcript of documentary film by Safaa Fathy, <http://www.lrc.edu/eng/Derrida/Elsewhere.htm> (1 October 2005).

come" of the future. For Derrida, it is always the ex-cess[56], or that which cannot be accounted for, totalized, absolutized, or subordinated to the unity of one, which gives us the possibility for justice, responsibility, hospitality and decision. Without a future to come, or without the excess of elsewhere, which constantly withdraws from presence and absolute appropriation, we have only the violence of totalization.

In a book entitled "A Taste for the Secret", Derrida states:

> I think that the instant one loses sight of the excess of justice, or of the future, in that very moment the conditions of totalization would, undoubtedly, be fulfilled – but so would the conditions of the totalitarianism of a right without justice, of a good moral conscience and a good juridical conscience, which all adds up to a present without a future.[57]

Totalization, in all its many forms, attempts to close down the future and give nothing other than what is and what is already known. It gives us a world of calculation and pre-existing knowledge in the here and now, but it cannot give us a future which holds the potentiality of an-other, a some-thing other, a thought not yet thought or determined by the present conditions. We see here why when Derrida speaks of democracy he says it is "to come." Democracy, as opposed to totalitarianism, needs a future that never absolutely arrives, for the moment it arrives, it is absolutely here and now, and not in the excess of elsewhere. The infinite arrival, the "to come", does not entail a passivity toward a working and striving toward a democratic state, it only recognizes that the notion of absolute arrival, an absolute here and now of a democracy without a future always to come,

---

[56] Here I am referring to Jean-Luc Nancy's analysis of the "ek" or "ex" which means "out of." For example, one could think of exposition as "out of" position. The important element I take from this notion is that the "ex" (out of) implies *movement* or an escape from that which attempts absolute appropriation.
[57] Jacques Derrida, and Maurizio Ferraris, *A Taste for the Secret*, trans. Giacomo Donis (Malden: Polity Blackwell Publishers, 2001), p. 22.

contains the seeds of totalized thinking. Democracy needs the "to come" of the future or it is not democracy.

Totalized thinking is fear of the future. It is a violent attempt to escape the temporality of "being-with" and becoming in the world. The attempt to close down time, the temporality of an always open future to come is an attempt to escape the always already uncertainty that prevails in every moment. All attempts at certainty through totalization are nothing other than attempts at freeing oneself from the uncertain terrain of being. In fact, this process is simply an attempt at freeing oneself from the aporia of such notions as decision and responsibility. In order to make a decision, or as Derrida would say any decision worthy of being called a free decision, it must first pass through the undecidable and thus uncertain space of aporetic temporality. For Derrida, the undecidable is the condition for decision, just as certain events are only possible as impossible. Here again we will listen to Derrida, a quote from the documentary:

> If there is decision and responsibility they should pass the test of aporia and the undecidable. From this moment – which is not just a phase, it is, in a way, an interminable moment – by the trial of this impossibility to decide or to dispose of a previously defined rule that would allow one to decide. In a certain way, I must, beyond all – "I musts" identifiable – not know where to go, not know what to do, not what I should decide, so that a decision – where it seems impossible – should be possible. - And therefore a responsibility.[58]

To not know, to not have the condition of calculability and certitude, is thus the space for a true decision to occur. If one knows where one is going, there is no need for decision, for it is simply a matter of following a path - a path not made by first being held in the uncertain space of aporia and indecision, but one made simply through an already known and thus

---

[58] "Derrida's Elsewhere," transcript of documentary film by Safaa Fathy, <http://www.lrc.edu/eng/Derrida/Elsewhere.htm> (1 October 2005).

determinable space. I quote Derrida again, this time from an essay/lecture entitled, "Force of Law: The 'Mystical Foundation of Authority'":

> A decision that didn't go through the ordeal of the undecidable would not be a free decision, it would only be a programmable application or unfolding of a calculable process. It might be legal; it would not be just.[59]

The "ordeal of the undecidable" is thus the space from which a true and free decision occurs. Without this aporetic space of uncertainty, there would be movements of thought in calculability, movements structured around preconditioned knowledge, but there would not be the absolute responsibility of making a decision when one does not know, or have access to previously known outcomes or conditions. In short, any decision, in the sense we are now discussing, is momentarily without measure. This decision without measure, this decision structured around undecidability, is a decision thus in excess or outside of being in general. It opens up, in its excess, the possibility of a world beyond calculation and totalization. The excess of decision in undecidabilty does not end once a decision is made, for as soon as a decision is made, it folds back into the aporia of future decisions. These decisions to come, decisions within undecidability and thus in excess of calculability, continue to give us a sense of space beyond totalization and absolutization. In other words, the decision to come gives us an elsewhere, an elsewhere outside the here and now, an elsewhere not reached or closed down by totalization. Elsewhere withdraws, it escapes totalized thinking in that it is also always already in excess of being found. In its withdrawal from totalization, elsewhere differs and defers from the here and now of being. Elsewhere is the excess of meaning, the "out-of" meaning, understood perhaps in the movement of Derrida's notion of *différance*.

---

[59] Jacques Derrida, "Force of Law: The 'Mystical Foundation of Authority'," in *Deconstruction and the Possibility of Justice*, edited by Drucilla Cornell and Michael Rosenfeld (New York: Routledge, 1992), p. 24.

I wish to emphasize here that the notion of undecidability does not in any way privilege endless deferral or resignation in regard to making a decision. It does not promote endless hesitation or rumination. The aporia of decision simply points to the responsibility of making a decision even though there is no absolute measure from which to verify its validity or outcome. A decision answers the obligation to act, to respond in the face of an indeterminable otherness, an unknown space open to the coming of that which is not yet known or understood. A decision furthermore has incredible transformative power; it opens the space for future being, becoming, and event. Its momentary passage (*poros*) through the aporia shifts the terrain of multiplicities and potentialities, and thus opens the world to an elsewhere always in flux and to come. A decision as such is the ethical possibility of being in the world. Without the uncertain space which precedes decision we would live in a static world of attempted certainty and totalization. We would live in a world without novelty and otherness. The uncertain steps and decisions ahead of us should not debilitate movement, but should pull us toward our ongoing and perhaps never ending ethical responsibility. The spatiality of an elsewhere and the temporality of a future "to come" may create an anxious and uncertain terrain for being, but they give life its potentiality in excess of totalization.

Being in itself is always in excess of itself. In other words, each and every being always holds in reserve a singularity which exceeds and therefore is "out of" any notion of entirety. In this sense, being is never a totalized one, nor an essence of oneness which precedes multiplicity. Being is multiple (Badiou) and each multiplicity shows or holds a singularity which exceeds the closure of absolute identity and identification. Here we can perhaps begin to understand Jean-Luc Nancy when he says that "being is singularly plural and plurally singular."[60] We can also sense how the relationship of unity to itself implies some element of difference, as Derrida states, for a being cannot simply be *one* with itself, or self-identical with itself. This pure oneness or unity is of course, death. Perhaps outside any

---

[60] Jean-Luc Nancy, *Being Singular Plural*, trans. Robert D. Richardson (Stanford: Stanford University Press, 2000), p. 28.

ontological or existential sense, and on strictly materialistic terms, we should also consider these notions in relation to the body, for the body is also always in a state of transformation. All forms of transformation need the movement of difference in relation to unity. Pure unity is simply without movement, change, and transformation, whether it be in the form of existential/ontological becoming or materialistic change. In other words, there is always some difference which is in excess of unity. In fact, this relation between difference and unity in itself is always a type of movement and motion, a differentiation we could in existential, ontological, and physical terms perhaps call life. The excess or "more than oneness" of being creates the "spacing"[61] and opening for a continuous becoming.

"I have a taste for the secret"[62] says Derrida in an interview by Maurizio Ferraris. Derrida has a taste for all things which are in excess of totalization. Furthermore, in the documentary, Derrida speaks of secrecy as "that which resists politics, that which resists politicization, citizenship, transparency, phenomenality."[63] In other words, the secret is that which is always outside, always out of and in excess of principles of organization, conceptualization, totalization and control. It resists the closure of pure identity or identification and accentuates the movement of difference. In its difference, as that which exceeds pure identity, the secret represents a non-totalized open space for a politics and ethics to come. Without the secret, or simply that which exceeds totalization, there is no democracy to come. A totalized society, a society closed down around a desire for oneness without difference and multiplicity, is a society without an elsewhere. The unreachable elsewhere draws thinking toward that which is not yet known, that uncertain and aporetic space left always open for future thought. The secret thus contains a secret in and of itself. The secret contains the secret of a future to come and an elsewhere that cannot be breached. Derrida's elsewhere, the elsewhere of Derrida, and

---

[61] This is a term used frequently by Derrida and Nancy. We will gain better insight into the term as the essay unfolds.

[62] Jacques Derrida, and Maurizio Ferraris, *A Taste for the Secret*, trans. Giacomo Donis (Malden: Polity Blackwell Publishers, 2001), p. 59.

[63] Source for transcript of film: http://www.lrc.edu/eng/Derrida/Elsewhere.htm

the elsewhere Derrida has given us to think, asks of us to think toward such notions as justice, decision, hospitality, and responsibility. It calls us toward thinking here and now, a here and now, however, always open to a non-totalized elsewhere and a future to come. Derrida's thinking asks us to think in the aporetic, undecidable, and uncertain space of being in a world, which is nothing other than being-with a world of multiple differential relations, and thus a world of continuous movement and negotiation through *différance*.

2.4 Différance: Movement/Spacing and the Possibility in Becoming

> Always differing and deferring, the trace is never as it is in the presentation of itself. It erases itself in presenting itself, muffles itself in resonating, like the *a* writing itself, inscribing its pyramid in *différance*.[64]
>
> - Jacques Derrida

> Thus, *différance* is the name we might give to the "active," moving discord of different forces, and of differences of forces, that Nietzsche sets up against the entire system of metaphysical grammar, wherever this system governs culture, philosophy, and science.[65]
>
> - Jacques Derrida

As a peripheral thought to our thinking and before our thinking on *différance*, I wish to momentarily place the phrase "as something is coming to be it is always already becoming something other" on the side or in the margins (Derrida) of our analysis. This statement will come back to us in full force as we think through *différance*, but for now it should perhaps stand

---

[64] Jacques Derrida, "*Différance*," chap. in *Margins of Philosophy* (Chicago: University of Chicago Press, 1986, c1982), p. 23.
[65] Derrida, "Difference," p. 18.

only as a reminder to our introductory remarks (sections 1.2, 1.3 and 1.4) which emphasized the becoming of being, the movement of becoming, and a becoming which furthermore displaces the linearity of cause and effect, and thus "origin." In short, our statement should for now, in the beginning of our analysis on *différance*, simply draw us toward thinking on the *activity* and *movement* implied in continuous becoming. Activity, movement, becoming... all of these and more, open us to the possibility of thinking the differing and deferring of *différance*, as opposed to a pure presence of being in itself as itself. To think *différance* we must orient our sensibility toward the incessant "between" – a transient space exceeding the structure of absolute binary opposition. As Derrida says in regard to *différance*, "It is more of the order of what is called the middle, in Greek grammar, neither passive nor active."[66] An activity, a motion, a happening in excess of the dialectical movement of binary opposition; *différance occurs*, or as Derrida would say, "takes place." *Différance*, in other words, deconstructs. But what does this mean?

In an interview with Raoul Mortley, Derrida is asked, as always, albeit in different ways, about deconstruction. Mortley begins by speaking of Plotinus, Neoplatonism, and in particular, the term *aphairesis* which etymologically means "to take away." More importantly, however, *aphairesis* implies that this "taking away" is done in order to find the real idea or truth beneath the layers. As Mortley points out, aphairetic thought functions in such a way as to emphasize the notion that "elements are removed from an idea to find its real kernel."[67] In short, *aphairesis* is usually understood as a process of removal, a step by step taking away, whereby a truth may be exposed. At any rate, after this description of *aphairesis*, Mortley asks Derrida if this "process of removal" is in any way analogous to deconstruction. Derrida's answer is "No." He, of course, goes on to say more, but the point to be made here is that deconstruction does not look for or attempt to uncover by means

---

[66] Raoul Mortley, "Interview with Jacques Derrida," chap. in *French Philosophers in Conversation* (London: Routledge, 1991), p. 99.
[67] Raoul Mortley, "Interview with Jacques Derrida," chap. in *French Philosophers in Conversation* (London: Routledge, 1991), p. 96.

of removal any such thing as truth or essence. There may be a "process," but most definitely not in order to find or discover some substance, truth, presence, real, or what have you, which lies beneath the many layers of "appearance." In fact, deconstruction in many ways shows that there is no fundamental essence to be found beneath the surface of appearance. The essence/appearance binary is simply a metaphysical construct, which by all means asks to be deconstructed itself. We can sense here why at times deconstruction may be at odds with certain elements in hermeneutics.[68] Deconstruction is not a process of unveiling in order to find a hidden meaning or truth, it more so asks why such a methodology of thinking occurs in the first place. What deconstruction also shows is that through a long history of metaphysics we have come to think in terms of not only binary opposition, but an opposition which always favors one side over the other. This is why we imagine and think according to the hermeneutic notion that perhaps through a continued analysis of various appearances, we will sooner or later find the essence or truth at hand. Deconstruction, on the other hand, happens ("takes place") within the oppositional structure itself. Doing so, it shows the resistance that occurs in an attempted unity, which in metaphysics, always tries to delineate itself from its polarized other. Deconstruction shows the very process by which binary opposition occurs. In other words, deconstruction takes place within structures, and furthermore shows the activity at work within them. Showing the activity from within the activity, deconstruction exposes the forces at play in metaphysical binary oppositional thinking. But deconstruction also exposes more; it also shows that in the midst of this binary schema there is an activity, a force at play, which Derrida calls "dissemination." This term draws us closer to our thinking on *différance*. In regard to the concept of dissemination Derrida states:

---

[68] For more on this issue see Diane P. Michelfelder, and Richard E. Palmer, *Dialogue and Deconstruction* (Albany: State University of New York Press, 1989). This book is made up of different texts surrounding "The Gadamer-Derrida Encounter."

The intention of this term is to emphasize the force of multiplication and dispersion, or of *différance*, a force which doesn't allow itself to be gathered or totalized.[69]

Deconstruction exposes the movement, motion, scattering, and "dispersion" of meaning within all attempts at totalized meaning. The movement and force of meaning (which resists the closure of absolutized unity) is dissemination. That which exceeds totalization, scatters itself about in a movement which refuses the ground or stability required for totalized meaning. This is why Derrida says, "Dissemination is something which no longer belongs to the regime of meaning; it exceeds not only the multiplicity of meanings, but also meaning itself."[70] How can dissemination exceed meaning itself? It does so by its never ending movement – its ongoing scattering which never finds a home in stabilized unity. In its continuous becoming, or its state of always already becoming other, it constantly "erases"[71] any sense of origin or stable meaning. We could already suggest here that *différance* disseminates, and deconstruction exposes or shows the disseminating movement of *différance*. In essence, dissemination exceeds the "regime of meaning" by being the groundless activity which in *différance* makes meaning possible. Dissemination can therefore never be exposed as meaning, for meaning relies fundamentally on a structure or topography of organized differences in relation to unity. Dissemination exceeds any topography in its incessant temporal and spatial dispersion and scattering. In this sense, dissemination, in its continuous movement as *différance*, creates the possibility for the unfolding of meaning and meanings to come. It cannot, however, in itself, be absolutely exposed or found as meaning itself. As Derrida states:

---

[69] Raoul Mortley, "Interview with Jacques Derrida," chap. in *French Philosophers in Conversation* (London: Routledge, 1991), p. 97.

[70] Mortley, "Interview with Jacques Derrida", p. 98.

[71] Here I am referring to Derrida's understanding of erasure. See in particular page 7 in *Of Grammatology*, trans. Gayatri Spivak (Baltimore: Johns Hopkins University Press, 1976).

> One can expose only that which at a certain
> moment can become present, manifest, that
> which can be shown, presented as something
> present, a being-present in its truth, in the truth
> of a present or the presence of the present.[72]

In its restless (Nancy) and continuous dispersion, dissemination exceeds being, or "being-present." It exceeds presence by the fact that it never stabilizes or stops, even for a moment, in order to show itself as this or that. Dissemination is the process of "as something is coming to be it is always already becoming other," for in each, there exists no moment of being-present, only a continuous activity of becoming. But here we must ask the question, what makes possible a continuous becoming and dissemination? What moves becoming? What disseminates? What makes for not only the possibility of meaning, but what is the condition of possibility as such? Here we will turn to the differing and deferring movement, or the "spacing" of *difference* itself.

From what we have already gathered in relation to deconstruction, dissemination, and becoming, it is clear that we cannot begin by asking the question, what "is" *différance*? We cannot ask what it "is" precisely because, as with dissemination, it exceeds the meaning of "being-present" or presence. *Différance* exceeds the logic of "is" altogether. As we have heard many times over, *différance* is "neither a word nor a concept."[73] But there is more. According to Derrida, the idea of *différance* is also "neither psychological, nor anthropological, nor phenomenological, nor ontological, in a certain sense."[74] Yes, in a certain sense *différance* is neither of the terms mentioned. So in what sense (Nancy) can we perhaps sense *différance*? First of all, we must not look toward what *différance* "is," but for what *différance* does. We must attempt to think an activity which "makes possible the presentation of

---

[72] Jacques Derrida, "*Différance*," chap. in *Margins of Philosophy* (Chicago: University of Chicago Press, 1986, c1982), p. 5-6.
[73] Derrida, "*Différance*," p. 3.
[74] Mortley, "Interview with Jacques Derrida," p. 101.

the being-present,"[75] as compared to thinking of *différance* as a presence in and of itself. We must think of what *différance* presents or "makes possible" instead of what *différance* represents. In other words, we must look toward an activity that makes possible such notions as ontology, phenomenology, hermeneutics, etc. In this sense, we are looking not for meaning itself, but for that which makes and creates the possibility of meaning. We are looking for an activity, which as Jean-Luc Nancy may say, makes sense by creating sense.[76] To a certain degree we are looking for that which produces sense, or that which makes possible the possibility for meaning. As Derrida states:

> The trace is in fact the absolute origin of sense in general. Which amounts to saying once again that there is no absolute origin of sense in general. The trace is the *différance* which opens appearance and signification.[77]

In *différance*, the trace gives meaning and sense, however, we must never think of trace or *différance* as absolute origin. Why? Because again, in its continuous becoming, in dissemination, trace and *différance*, "erase" any sense of origin and meaning in and of themselves. We can perhaps say here that *différance* moves in a simultaneous trace-erase manner, all the time opening the space for possible "appearance and signification." It is with these factors in mind that we gain insight into what *différance does*, as compared to what it may or may not be as in representation. So how does *différance* go about creating the possibility of meaning and sense? And, is perhaps *différance* nothing other than the condition of possibility itself? Is *différance* that which makes possible possibility itself? We shall see.

---

[75] Derrida, "*Différance*," p. 6.
[76] Here I am playing off Jean-Luc Nancy's notion of "sense."
[77] Jacques Derrida, *Of Grammatology*, trans. Gayatri Spivak (Baltimore: Johns Hopkins University Press, 1976), p. 65.

To get a closer look at what *différance does*, we should look now at the double gesture implied in the term. As Derrida tells us, the verb *differer* (from the Latin verb *differre*) has two meanings. Both meanings found in one word are distinct from one another in the sense that one meaning is "to defer" and the other is "to differ". To differ is of course to be not the same, or "to be not identical, to be other, discernible, etc."[78] It is to be different in all senses of the word. To defer, on the other hand, suggests a relation to time, or as Derrida says "temporization." In this sense, to defer means a type of delay, a waiting, a temporary moment of suspension. To defer is to not demand absolute immediacy. It is a momentary temporal "holding back" which functions in correlation with the desire for such things as completion. So, as we can see here, one word (*differre*) with two different and distinct meanings – to differ and to defer. What Derrida accomplishes with *différance* (with an "a") is a gesture for thinking the possibility of both (differ and defer) at the same time. In Derrida's words, "*différance* can refer simultaneously to the entire configuration of its meanings."[79]

Différance is thus to differ and to defer, or better yet, it "takes place" in a simultaneous activity of differing and deferring. Differences create deferral and deferral creates differences. By differing, difference opens the space for temporal delay and deferral. Furthermore, this deferral in itself, maintains the structure of differentiation. It does so by keeping open the space of difference. Absolute immediacy, or an absolute lack of any deferral whatsoever, is the absolute closure of the same. In concrete terms, being different from someone or something always contains an element of deferral, for absolute immediacy would translate into an absolute merging into the sameness of one. Difference is maintained by deferral and deferral is maintained by difference. Difference is deferral and deferral is difference - together in play at the same time - *différance*. It is here that we can understand what *différance does*, or how *différance* creates by way of the differing and deferring movement of spacing. Spacing is in itself the temporal and spatial movement of becoming. As Derrida states:

---

[78] Derrida, "*Différance*," p. 8.
[79] Derrida, "*Différance*," p. 8.

I often talk about spacing, but this is not simply space as opposed to time, but a mode of producing space by temporalizing it (*en le temps-poralisant*). Temporization, to temporize, means waiting or expecting (*attendre*), postponing or delaying. Temporizing is spacing by way of making an interval, and here again with the idea of difference the ideas of spacing and temporization are inextricably linked.[80]

As we can see, spacing *creates* an interval, a gap between differences in deferral. In the differing and deferring play, a multiplicity of possibilities for meaning and sense unfold. *Différance* opens the space for sense and meaning; it produces the possibility for the multiplicity[81] (Badiou) of possibilities to come. We see here how *différance* is not ontology, phenomenology, etc., for *différance* is the condition for their possibility. In the movement of spacing, *différance* makes space and thus also its correlate - time. It would be tempting here to suggest that *différance* is the source or motor of all becoming, the source for a movement of "as something is coming to be it is always already becoming something other." But here we would have to think of "source" as the ungrounded multiplicity of possibility without origin. It is perhaps better to think of *différance* as the condition of possibility itself. As such, *différance* spaces, defers, differs, traces, erases, disseminates, deconstructs, and so on, in an endless movement of being-between and anxious becoming.

2.5 The Milieu of Undecidability

Then, in the second place, the responsibility of what remains to be decided, or done (in actuality) cannot consist in following, applying,

---

[80] Mortley, "Interview with Jacques Derrida," p. 100.
[81] Throughout the essay, I periodically use the term "multiplicity." I am using the term in reference to and in recognition of Alain Badiou's thinking on this concept. For Badiou, being is multiple.

or realizing a norm or rule. When there is a
determinable rule, I know what must be done,
and as soon as such knowledge dictates the law,
action follows knowledge as a calculable
consequence: one *knows* what path to take, one
no longer hesitates; the decision then no longer
decides anything but simply gets deployed with
the automatism attributed to machines.[82]

- Jacques Derrida

Nietzsche's philosophy of becoming and event disavows the
temporality and phenomenological binary structure of cause and
effect, or, to use Derrida's words in the quote above, "action"
and "consequence." Movement and change seen simply along
the lines of a causal chain, for Nietzsche, is nothing other than
an imposition, inference, or limitation in understanding
"activity" itself. Division, and the act of demarcation where
cause stands *absolutely* separate from effect, leads to a linear
(teleological) thinking closed off from accepting the complexity
of activity or the phenomena of becoming. This is not to say
that events do not occur in any manner according to causes and
effects; it is more so an understanding that there is always some
cause in effect and some effect in cause. In other words, they
intermingle. They are parts of one another in an incessant
movement of transformation and activity. Between them exists
a temporal space of transference – a space also not separate or
divided, but interwoven into the interstitial activity. As
Nietzsche states:

The "evolution" of a thing, a custom, an organ is
thus by no means its *progressus* toward a goal,
even less a logical *progressus* by the shortest
route and with the smallest expenditure of force
– but a succession of more or less mutually
independent processes of subduing, plus the

---

[82] Giovanna Borradori, *Philosophy in a Time of Terror: Dialogues with Jurgen Habermas and Jacques Derrida* (Chicago: University of Chicago Press, 2003), p. 134.

resistances they encounter, the attempts at transformation for the purpose of defense and reaction, and the results of successful counteractions.[83]

Later on in the same aphorism, Nietzsche names this activity the "will to power." He uses this phrase in many different contexts throughout his works, each time attempting to describe the phenomena in various ways. In this sense, the concept of will to power, throughout all its differential descriptions, names and marks a limit in descriptive language. The words together as a phrase attempt to speak of an activity or event of becoming, yet, while spoken or written, the phrase always risks falling into the metaphysical logic of language. Nietzsche knows this. When speaking of lightning and flash, he shows us how the mind posits the former as cause and the latter as the effect. Again, for Nietzsche, they are one and the same – neither cause nor effect, but an activity only *described* in such terms. To speak and thus to think along the logic of subject as cause and verb as effect, misses the infinite series and degrees of happenings *between* the lines of any phenomenological occurrence. Furthermore, it is not simply the logic of one thing leading to another thing in a linear or teleological fashion, but a complex system of interactivity where various forces cross in interstitial play. As Nietzsche states, "there is no 'being' behind doing, effecting, becoming; 'the doer' is merely a fiction added to the deed – the deed is everything."[84] We see that for Nietzsche there is only a becoming, an endless movement or activity which cannot be captured by the logic and metaphysical structure of language. It seems the world as will to power can only be expressed in different contexts as *movement*, where such notions as subject and object stand as a multiplicity of relations in relation to this ongoing activity. With this in mind, the transitory "to" which stands between the "will" and "power," seems of utmost importance. The "will" stands in relation to a multiplicity of other active and reactive wills, and "power" names not a stable

[83] Friedrich Nietzsche, *On the Genealogy of Morals and Ecce Homo*, trans. Walter Kaufman and R.J. Hollingdale (New York: Random House, 1967), p. 77.
[84] Ibid., p. 45.

end or goal in itself but the force or activity from which
becoming emerges. Again, one must sense the importance of the
"to" in this phrase, for it alone captures the space *between*
relations, or the spacing of differentiation, and thus furthermore
highlights the "activity" that Nietzsche is attempting to describe.
This movement and activity of becoming as will to power is
therefore not a binary dialectical movement, but a transformation
made up of multiplicities of interstitial relations – an entangled
web of activity without any particular goal or direction in mind.
As Nietzsche states in regard to all movement and
transformation, "The form is fluid, but the 'meaning' is even
more so."[85]

The fluid space of transformation (transvaluation) thus
described above and named "will to power" by Nietzsche,
resembles and is analogous to the aporetic space of the
"undecidable" utilized in the philosophy of Derrida. It shares a
structural ambiguity and an ambiguity within its differential and
multiple relations. For Derrida, a responsible or ethical decision
does not occur inside the stream of causal logic, or as Derrida
states above where "action follows knowledge," but according to
the non-knowledge or uncertainty that surrounds the event. To
decide in the structure of undecidability as compared to
knowledge and calculability is to decide in the realm of the
uncertain and complex interactivity of ongoing differential
relations. In other words, it is to decide in the aporetic structure
of becoming as compared to the linear structure of cause and
effect. In this sense (and here to emphasize the "structural"
similarities of the will to power and the undecidable space for
decision), the will to power as becoming stands not as a
direction or goal, but as the undecidable space from which an
ethical decision may emerge. The will to power is the uncertain,
enigmatic, and ambiguous transformative space from which the
responsibility for decision is not determined by the
"automatism" of knowledge and certitude, but by the risk or
"leap of faith" (Kierkegaard) entailed in any true decision.
Against the interpretation of Heidegger, Nietzsche's "will to
power" as concept, does not stand within the metaphysics of

---

[85] Ibid., p. 78.

subject or subjectness[86], but orients our thinking toward a space where transformations in and of thinking (and thus decisions) take place. The will to power is the contingent milieu from which events occur. Within this space, which is the world (as Nietzsche says, "this world is the will to power - and nothing besides!"[87]) one must decide within nothing other than multiplicity, continuous becoming as transformation, and thus, contingent undecidability.

To live in pseudo certainty (I say pseudo because one can never be absolutely certain) is an attempt at freeing oneself from the anxiety of not-knowing. Life gives itself to us and unfolds a multiplicity of events which surround us in an impossible space of differential relations. What we make of this always already space of uncertainty is our ethical possibility. If one moves out of this realm with quick and solid notions of certitude, one simply stands outside the necessary and constant fluctuations that make up the ambiguous terrain which precedes all decisions. In an attempt at certainty, one simply separates oneself from the aporia that precedes decision, or, as Derrida would say "the ghost of the undecidable." The quest for certainty is an attempt to release oneself from the anxious haunting that forever calls us into the impossibility of ever knowing for sure that we did the right thing or made the right decision. In fact, we are always already in the undecidable even when we make a decision, for as soon as the decision is made we fold back into the impossibility of being finished with new decisions. Undecidability surrounds each and every decision. It is not an either/or situation where one is either in a decision or in undecidability. One is in both simultaneously. Furthermore, undecidability is not between two conflicting decisions. As Derrida states:

> The undecidable is not merely the oscillation or
> the tension between two decisions; it is the
> experience of that which, though heterogeneous,
> foreign to the order of the calculable and the

---

[86] See volumes 1-4 entitled "Nietzsche" and the essay "The Word of Nietzsche: 'God is Dead'" by Heidegger.
[87] Friedrich Nietzsche, *The Will to Power*, trans. Walter Kaufman and R.J. Hollingdale (New York: Vintage Books, 1968), p. 550.

> rule, is still obliged – it is of obligation that we
> must speak – to give itself up to the impossible
> decision, while taking account of law and rules.
> A decision that did not go through the ordeal of
> the undecidable would not be a free decision, it
> would only be a programmable application or
> unfolding of a calculable process. It might be
> legal; it would not be just.[88]

The "ordeal of the undecidable" is the space from which a decision may emerge, yet, after the decision is made, one is not simply done with the undecidable. The momentary passage (*poros*) of the decision stays intimately entwined with the undecidable, for as quick as the decision cuts through the fabric of undecidability, it as quickly exposes itself to new and unfinished decisions to come. As Derrida says above, the undecidable is not "merely the oscillation or the tension between two decisions," but more so an obligation to make a decision, albeit one that it is structured around an impossible completion or certainty. The undecidable is not the space between the two or many, but a structurally entwined phenomenon, which in a Deleuzian manner, temporally folds and unfolds the act of decision back and forth into existence. This is why Derrida stresses the haunting or ghostlike structure of the undecidable. It is always there, in every decision, whether one chooses to see it or not. It calls the decision back into undecidability. This does not mean, however, that a decision lacks transformative power.

In essence, a decision structured around undecidability opens the transformative space of becoming and event. It momentarily reorients the interwoven terrain of multiplicities and potentialities for an event not known, but to come. This decision thus marks the ethical possibility and opening for continuous transformation in any realm, whether in law, justice, responsibility, or politics. Without the uncertain transformative space (the "will to power" for Nietzsche and the "undecidable" for Derrida) which precedes decision, we live only in the

---

[88] Jacques Derrida, "Force of Law: The 'Mystical Foundation of Authority'," in *Deconstruction and the Possibility of Justice*, edited by Drucilla Cornell and Michael Rosenfeld (New York: Routledge, 1992), p. 24.

movements of determined determination, which never allow the possibility of an unknown coming or event unbeknownst to the knowledge of the day. In short, with only certainty and knowledge as our guide, very little in this world would change. We would live in a world closed down to the novelty of an event – a rupture always necessarily outside the limits of knowledge and current logic. Maintaining uncertainty does not lead to endless deferral or hesitation, but to a decision which first and foremost answers the obligation to act, and secondly always falls back immediately into the reoriented and restructured terrain of undecidability. Every decision reorganizes the fabric of life, but each move in itself does not lead to a conclusive point of certainty; it leads to a new, uncertain, undecidable, and aporetic space from which once again we must decide and act. The uncertain steps ahead of us do not debilitate movement; they pull us toward an impossible completion of thinking and being. This impossibility coupled with the uncertainty that keeps it alive, allows a space for being and becoming outside the regime of totalized thought.

2.6 Decision within Indecision

> When there is no *double-bind*, there is no responsibility.[89]
>
> - Jacques Derrida

> The simple concepts of alterity and of singularity constitute the concept of duty as much as that of responsibility. As a result, the concepts of responsibility, of decision, or of duty, are condemned a priori to paradox, scandal, and aporia.[90]
>
> - Jacques Derrida

---

[89] Jacques Derrida, and Bernard Stiegler, *Echographies of Television*, trans. Jennifer Bajorek (Cambridge: Polity Press, 2002), p. 26.
[90] Jacques Derrida, *The Gift of Death*, trans. David Wills (Chicago: University of Chicago Press, 1995), p. 68.

What is a decision? What is the mark, the interruption, the gesture which temporarily breaks through the indecisive and aporetic space of uncertainty? Phenomenologically speaking, what is the spatio-temporal fabric upon which the stitch of decision is sewn? If one decides, or chooses one particular entity over another, is this act not hegemonic through and through? How can one choose anything, decide anything, without sensing the absolute moment of demarcation – a closing off (temporarily) of all other others? Each and every instant of every decision, large or small, brings with it reverberations beyond knowledge and certainty. Metaphorically speaking, if one chooses to go left as compared to right (not to mention the multiplicity of degrees between them, and between these degrees more infinitesimal spaces of difference) one simultaneously opens a space for more decisions to come and closes forever the space of all the other momentary possibilities lost. The constant and simultaneous opening/closure of all the various possibilities around the act of decision creates the interstitial web from which we weave our lives. Each instant contains a multiplicity of possibilities and *at the same time* a multiplicity of forever lost potentialities. An opening created by a decision creates the space for another decision and so on. A decision, therefore, may be viewed analogously to a temporary *poros* or passage as discussed in section 2.1. For emphasis and further analysis, I will bring us back to the essential quote where Sarah Kofman states:

> *Poros* refers only to a sea-route or route down a river, to a passage opened up across a chaotic expanse which it transforms into an ordered, qualified space by introducing differentiated routes, making visible the various directions of space, by giving direction to an expanse which was initially devoid of all contours, of all landmarks.[91]

---

[91] Sarah Kofman, "Beyond Aporia?," in *Post-Structuralist Classics*, ed. Andrew Benjamin (New York: Routledge, 1988), p. 10.

The *poros* (decision) being represented as a sea-route wonderfully expresses the interconnectivity of past and future events which make up each and every decision or passage. The decision, in other words, is always already in motion in relation to the past and what is to come. The aporetic or "chaotic expanse" is momentarily given a shape/"contour" from which the decision not only creates direction, but simultaneously finds direction. Each decision finds itself between a past from which it originated and a future that awaits its origination. But each decision, opening, or temporary passage, also leaves behind a multiplicity of pathways forever unknown. The moment a decision is made, it closes off forever, spaces of possibility never to be known. The traces (Derrida) left at each and every point, every pivot point of the opening/closure of decision, mark the enigmatic and aporetic space from which we attempt to move through life. The always already uncertainty of ceaseless becoming is the ontological condition from which decisions are made. Being caught up or "condemned" to this paradoxical and aporetic state which precedes decision, does not promote indecision; it in fact, as Derrida emphasizes, allows a true decision to occur. The moment of decision, in other words, is fundamentally structured around an *a priori* sense of indecision. Without indecision, and thus uncertainty, there is no true decision.

Further on in the same text, Derrida speaks of Abraham, or, we should say Kierkegaard's interpretation of the biblical story of Abraham and Isaac. Derrida states:

> Abraham doesn't speak in figures, fables, parables, metaphors, ellipses, or enigmas. His irony is meta-rhetorical. If he knew what was going to happen, if for example God had charged him with the mission of leading Isaac onto the mountain so that he could strike him with lightning, then he would have been right to have recourse to enigmatic language. But the problem is precisely that he doesn't know. Not that that makes him hesitate, however. His nonknowledge doesn't in any way suspend his

own decision, which remains resolute. The knight of faith must not hesitate. He accepts his responsibility by heading off towards the absolute request of the other, beyond knowledge. He decides, but his absolute decision is neither guided nor controlled by knowledge. Such, in fact, is the paradoxical condition of every decision: it cannot be deduced from a form of knowledge of which it would simply be the effect, conclusion, or explicitation.[92]

We see again that a decision is marked not by knowledge or certainty, but by the very "nonknowledge" and uncertainty of the conditions that make up a particular situation. The call and request of the other brings one toward the impossible paradoxical threshold which structures every decision, i.e., if one chooses one direction, temporarily all other directions are closed off and thus left irresponsibly alone. As one can see, responsibility and irresponsibility are tightly interwoven in the structure of decision making. As Derrida says,

> I can respond only to the one (or to the One), that is, to the other, by sacrificing that one to the other. I am responsible to any one (that is to say to any other) only by failing in my responsibility to all the others, to the ethical or political generality.[93]

What should one make of this paradoxical and impossible responsibility? What choices should be made when all along one knows that others are left calling, unseen, unrecognized, and unheard? Choice forces us into a "double bind," an enigmatic moment, an aporia where one cannot not respond, yet in the midst of this response ever say with a quick brush of the hand, "I am done." There is a never ending call, yet one of the ones, one of the singularities in front of us, must be reckoned with. To be

---

[92] Jacques Derrida, *The Gift of Death*, trans. David Wills (Chicago: University of Chicago Press, 1995), p. 77.
[93] Ibid., p. 70.

responsible we must decide on something. We must choose and make a decision, but we are also tangled up in the inability to choose everything and all at the same instant. In fact, choosing everything at the same instant is a contradiction in terms, for choice in itself is always structured *momentarily*[94] in the hegemony of deciding on a singular and particular one. We may choose a many or a multiplicity, but in the act, in the moment of decision, this multiple is a multiple unity. In other words, the multiplicity chosen is still demarcated from other multiplicities, thus simply one "particular-chosen-multiplicity" amongst others. Again, we simply cannot choose *everything and all* in the same temporal moment of decision, thus we are forever bound to its aporetic structure.   This aporetic structure demands that we maintain and continue to retreat into the realm of the uncertain, for any decision which attempts to stay within the certain, promotes a totalized/absolutized closure more drastic than the original closure implied in the hegemony of all decision making. The longer a decision remains rooted in certainty, the more so it closes off the possibility of re-evaluation and thus other openings for another other. This opening for re-evaluation does not necessarily mean an opening to an-other other (although it may), but perhaps the otherness, alterity, and difference of the other already at hand. In short, there is always the possibility of otherness within an already chosen other, and there is furthermore an always already otherness of self in becoming. To be open to the other, the other which fundamentally is and continuously maintains difference, is to see the multiplicity of otherness which surrounds us, whether this be inside or outside our becoming in and with the world. It is to recognize being, becoming, and otherness as *différance* (Derrida) – the continuous movement and spacing which creates and transforms our world. In its movement, *différance* opens the world to its uncertain trajectory, and in its spacing, it ex-poses the world to

---

[94] I wish to emphasize "momentarily," for even though the act of decision needs this temporary rupture into a type of certainty (perhaps here a look at Alain Badiou's notion of fidelity would be helpful), it is necessary to fall back into uncertainty before the decision ever manifests or solidifies into a dogmatic absolute, thus not open to the transformative power of re-interpretation and new openings for decisions to come.

its "uncertainty as such."[95] Right next to this, however, is the necessary and momentary break from the suspended space of indecision (the space where *all* others are calling, where *all* voices are heard) – the break into a singular decision. As Derrida points out with the words of Kierkegaard, "the instant of decision is madness."[96] The madness exists not only in the multiplicity of voices which call us toward them as others, but in the paradox of the instant, where one opening from decision only leaves another and many others closed. The "moment" or "instant" within temporality itself contains the kernel of madness. The paradox of decision and responsibility lays bare and exposes the "restlessness"[97] and anxiety of being in a world, which as Jean-Luc Nancy states, is nothing other than "being-with-one-another, circulating in the *with* and the *with* of this singularly plural coexistence."[98] The *being-with* of being demands decision within the impossible space of indecision.

---

[95] In regard to the "uncertainty as such" of our world, I am referring to a passage from: Jean-Luc Nancy, "What is to be Done?," in *Deconstruction: A Reader*, ed. Martin McQuillan (New York: Routledge, 2001), p. 457.

[96] Jacques Derrida, *The Gift of Death*, trans. David Wills (Chicago: University of Chicago Press, 1995), p. 65.

[97] Here I am referring to Jean-Luc Nancy, *Hegel: The Restlessness of the Negative*, trans. Jason Smith and Steven Miller (Minneapolis: University of Minnesota Press, 2002)

[98] Jean-Luc Nancy, *Being Singular Plural*, trans. Robert D. Richardson and Anne E. O'Byrne (Stanford: Stanford University Press, 2000), p. 3.

Part 3: Uncertainty as the Opening for Thinking to Come: Jean-Luc Nancy

3.1 Openings: Be-Coming Comes

> It is probably even through the process of discerning the themes and structures of the "closed upon itself" that one may begin to make oneself available to the "open," to what comes – to that which, since it comes and since its essence lies in coming, in the yet-to-come, it has no "self" upon which to close itself.[99]
>
> - Jean-Luc Nancy

By all means, it is better to have an "open mind" than a "closed mind," but is an "open mind" truly open? What is an "open mind" open to? Is it open to some-thing, some pre-thought idea or notion, or is it open to nothing in particular? The difference here makes all the difference. Let's take a look at why.

In section 2.2 "A Future To-Come," we saw the importance of indeterminacy in relation to the coming of that which is absolutely other. We recognized that Derrida's notion of "to-come" relies on a lack of determination and predetermination in regard to the possible "*arrivant*," or the arrival of the other as other. The arrival of an absolute other cannot by definition be expected or predetermined; the other must exceed any and all determinations, otherwise it is simply the already here endorsement or recognition of the same. This is why Derrida has a problem with the philosophical notion of horizon, for even here, in this space for thinking, there is an element of predetermination. As Derrida states:

---

[99] Jean-Luc Nancy, *The Gravity of Thought*, trans. Francois Raffoul and Gregory Recco (Atlantic Highlands: Humanities Press, 1997), p. 11.

> It is perhaps necessary to free the value of the
> future from the value of 'horizon' that
> traditionally has been attached to it – a horizon
> being – as the Greek word indicates, a limit from
> which I pre-comprehend the future.[100]

The pre-comprehension of horizon in itself closes the possibility of the coming of other as difference. Again, for Derrida, the "to come" must always remain absolutely ungrounded, indeterminable, and therefore always open. This "open" space for the "to come" of difference and other, is "open" not in a determinate manner, i.e., open to this or that, but open as ungrounded indeterminacy itself. In short, the "open" is the opening to come and the "to come" which is always open.

We can sense here the difference between an "open mind"[101] and that of the opening or open space for a thinking to come. An "open mind" is open to some predetermined entity or another, whereas the open space for the coming of the other is always indeterminate and thus open only as an opening. The opening is not a horizon, but a space of indeterminacy from which the otherness of other may come. For Nancy, this opening is the space for meaning and sense. Meaning comes, it arrives not "from an openness *of* thought"[102] where openness implies some sort of precondition, but from the opening of a space for thought itself – the opening to come. Nancy states:

> The dimension of the open, then, is the one
> according to which nothing (nothing essential) is
> established or settled; it is the one according to
> which everything essential *comes to be*.[103]

---

[100] Jacques Derrida, and Maurizio Ferraris, *A Taste for the Secret*, trans. Giacomo Donis (Malden: Polity Blackwell Publishers, 2001), p. 20.

[101] Here I am also referring to a gesture by Nancy, where in the Introduction to *The Gravity of Thought*, he points out the difference between "openness" as in being liberal, etc., as compared to the opening of thought itself, or, "thought as the opening."

[102] Jean-Luc Nancy, *The Gravity of Thought*, trans. Francois Raffoul and Gregory Recco (Atlantic Highlands: Humanities Press, 1997), p. 10.

[103] Ibid

As we can see, nothing "established" or "settled" can come because it is already recognized and determined as such. Coming needs the unknown and uncertain - the undetermined opening for arrival. Something essential may come to be, but the characteristics or nature of its essentiality must remain undetermined. One could say here that its activity of "coming to be" must never end; its movement must never halt in the stability of absolute and totalized recognition. In order for a continuous coming, and therefore a continuous be-coming, there need be a destabilized element which is in excess of any attempted unity. There need be an element which exceeds determinacy altogether. For Nancy and Derrida, this is nothing other than the absolute difference implied in the notion of singularity – the heterogeneous and irreducible other as absolutely other. As Derrida says, "That which defies anticipation, reappropriation, calculation – any form of pre-determination – is singularity."[104] Singularity thus opens and keeps open the "to come" of the future. It allows meaning and sense to continuously arrive in the opening and space left open by difference, *différance*, and singularity. This opening, for Nancy, is our opening to the "sense of the world" – the space where meaning comes and be-comes possible. It is not the space to stabilize or "pin down" meaning, but the space left open for meaning and meanings to come. Meaning *"comes to be"* and any signification comes afterward. To mark this difference in meaning Nancy states: "For signification is located meaning, while meaning resides perhaps only in the coming of a possible signification."[105] Meaning thus comes, be-comes, and continues to come, in the opening of the "to come". Signification, however, comes afterward in identification and recognition. It is the meaning we place on meaning after it arrives. Signification is possible through our various desires and determination, whereas meaning as that which arrives, comes outside our prediction and hitherto knowledge. It comes in the continuous becoming of being and world, in perhaps the unpredictable movement and spacing of *différance*. Openings as becoming and becoming as openings, the meaning and meanings of and in the world unfold. Be-

[104] Derrida, *A Taste for the Secret*, p. 21.
[105] Nancy, *The Gravity of Thought*, p. 10.

coming, as the continuous coming of singular being, comes in the opening of indeterminacy itself.

3.2 On Being-With and Being Singular Plural

> On the basis of this *like-with* being-in-the-world, the world is always already the one that I share with the others. The world of *Da-sein* is a *with-world*. Being-in is *being-with* others. The innerworldly being-in-itself of others is *Mitda-sein*.[106]
>
> - Martin Heidegger

> Being cannot *be* anything but being-with-one-another, circulating in the *with* and as the *with* of this singularly plural coexistence.[107]
>
> - Jean-Luc Nancy

After Nietzsche's philosophy, the question "who am I?" becomes more so the question of "who are 'we'?" Nietzsche's thinking in various ways exposes us to a multiplicity of being – a multiplicity of subject, subjectivity, self and selves. What Nietzsche draws us toward is an understanding of subject not as a unity or totalized identity, but a subject understood as a plurality. Nancy sums up this plural or multiple subject with the phrase "ego sum = ego cum."[108] The ego (subject) is not alone even by itself, or in itself; it is always already *with* itself as multiple selves. In other contexts, which include not only the plurality of other selves with self, but the self in relation to other others outside the self, Nancy thinks through this plurality as a

---

[106] Martin Heidegger, *Being and Time*, trans. Joan Stambaugh (Albany: State University of New York Press, 1996), p. 111-112. Here is not the place to go into a lengthy analysis of Heidegger's notion of *Mitsein*. I only place the quote here as a reference to Nancy's thinking on this term.

[107] Jean-Luc Nancy, *Being Singular Plural*, trans. Robert D. Richardson and Anne E. O'Byrne (Stanford: Stanford University Press, 2000), p. 3.

[108] Jean-Luc Nancy, *Being Singular Plural*, trans. Robert D. Richardson and Anne E. O'Byrne (Stanford: Stanford University Press, 2000), p. 31.

"we." Combining both aspects of plural being, the "we" here represents a plurality of self *with* other others, *and* a plurality of other selves *with* self. In the latter case, it is the be-coming of self, the movement and spacing of oneself in differentiation to the other-self that was and is to come. In the former case, it is a matter of becoming in relation to the difference of an-other outside the self. Of course, in becoming, we cannot separate the two; they interact and are always at play with one another. In short, we are always becoming, and thus becoming other, in relation to the otherness of other selves and other others. As Nancy says, "'I am' now, not the same as 'I was' yesterday."[109] What we have here is a two-fold sense of multiple becoming, a "we" of becoming in relation to self and others. In this sense, the "we" exceeds any stabilization or totalized unity.

As we saw in section 2.4, becoming becomes through the movement and spacing of *différance*; it is a movement and production in and of dissemination. This scattering of difference makes up the space and time of what Nancy calls the "with" or the "being-with" of being and existence. As Nancy states:

> "With" is the sharing of time-space; it is the at-the-same-time-in-the-same-place as itself, in itself, shattered. It is the instant scaling back of the principle of identity: Being is at the same time in the same place only on the condition of the spacing of an indefinite plurality of singularities.[110]

As we can see, being-with is a sharing, but not a sharing which moves toward such notions as identity, "community,"[111] or organization. These terms imply a coming together of that which is the same, or a sense of shared similarities as in traits, characteristics, etc. The sharing implied by Nancy is a sharing of singularities – a sharing of the irreducible otherness of each and every singularity itself. Each and every singularity together

---

[109] See appendix (section 1).
[110] Nancy, *Being Singular Plural*, p. 35.
[111] For more on Nancy's thinking on community see Jean-Luc Nancy, *The Inoperative Community* (Minneapolis: University of Minnesota Press, 1991).

forms a plurality of singularities. Each singularity *with* another, or as Nancy says, the "one + one + one…"[112] of singularities, makes up the "singularly plural and plurally singular"[113] notion of being in the world. Being together in the plurality of singular being, for Nancy, is not a union, communion, or merging of any sort. It more so suggests a side by side relation where singularities do not merge into identities or communities of the same, but into pluralities of singular difference. Differing (and deferring) singularities move in a continuous relation of being in differentiation. This is the "circulation" Nancy speaks of in being-with. In this sense, the "with" of "being-with," functions as a type of indeterminate space for becoming, coming to be, and the "being-toward"[114] of transformative being. Being-with is by all means a relation to difference, a relation *toward* that which is not the same. The same, or absolute unity in itself, has no movement or becoming, for it exists "in itself," by itself, and only for itself. Having no other of itself or to itself, it exists in the immobility of its own absolute being. Quite simply, there is no "with" of a totalized same. The "with" of being is the movement of being, or the being-toward which accentuates the space of being-between. We are always between being, in the sense that we never absolutely arrive as stabilized unity or identity. Being between is not simply the space between this and that, but the opening itself from which being as becoming unfolds. As Nancy states: "The 'between' is the stretching out [*distension*] and distance opened by the singular as such, as its spacing of meaning."[115] The spacing of singular (and plural) being therefore opens up the "between" of continuous becoming. Moving always in the between and toward, we are always "circulating in the *with*." This circulation is the becoming of

---

[112] See appendix (section 1).

[113] Nancy, *Being Singular Plural*, p. 28.

[114] Nancy uses this Heideggerian phrase "being-toward" [*l'etre-a*] to emphasize a movement in meaning and being in contrast to "being-such" [*l'etre-tel*]. From this I tend emphasize the movement of "being-toward" with that implied in becoming. The next section will discuss this in more detail, but for a clear example of Nancy's usage of these terms see Jean-Luc Nancy, *The Sense of the World*, trans. Jeffrey S. Librett (Minneapolis: University of Minnesota Press, 1997), p. 12.

[115] Nancy, *Being Singular Plural*, p. 5.

being, where becoming becomes and comes to be in being-with. This singular plural sharing of world is the becoming of world. It is the space and opening for our "sense of the world." Perhaps, the being-with of singular plural being is nothing other than the becoming of/in becoming itself, the instant which at each moment is and also is not. As Nancy says, "We are each time an other, each time with others."[116] In short, each and every time in becoming, be-coming becomes. Becoming occurs in the "with" of being.

3.3 Sense and World

> Sense no longer offers itself in the religious bond of a community, and knowledge is no longer organized into a meaningful totality. But community gives way to society – which, from now on, knows itself as separated from itself – and knowledge is the knowledge of objects and procedures, none of which is an end in itself. This world perceives itself as the gray world of interests, oppositions, particularities, and instrumentalities. It therefore perceives itself as a world of separation and of pain, a world whose history is of one atrocity after another, and whose consciousness is the consciousness of a constitutive unhappiness.[117]
>
> - Jean-Luc Nancy

If one feels separated from oneself, one usually speaks of a type of unhappiness or depression organized around such concepts as lack and displacement. One feels "empty" or "out of place." It is a feeling of not only being out of place in the world or in relation to the world, but also out of place with oneself as such. The sense of being out of place with oneself is structured

---

[116] Ibid, p. 35.
[117] Jean-Luc Nancy, *Hegel: The Restlessness of the Negative*, trans. Jason Smith and Steven Miller (Minneapolis: University of Minnesota Press, 2002), p. 3.

around the notion that one is separated from oneself – separated, in other words, from the self one imagines oneself to ("really and truly") be. In short, one has an idea or idealization of what one "really" is, or supposed to be, and then finds oneself in a position in life which is at odds or in contradistinction to this supposed self. It is felt or sensed that one's "true" being has either been left behind, or is not yet here or to be. This split, this gap between a present self in relation to an imagined self, is one source of a continued movement through life in unhappiness. Living life in such a manner is living a life in continuous separation from oneself. It is a constant movement through life where being here or there always translates into the thought that one really should be somewhere else, whether in a career, relationship, "place in life," etc. What is fundamentally at issue here, and furthermore, the source of the problem, is the preconceived and false notion that there is any such thing as a substantial or true self.   The continuous becoming and displacement of being is not a problem in itself, it only becomes a problem (and thus a possible source of unhappiness) if one imagines a true self at all times lingering behind or waiting in front of the becoming self. The problem is not the continuous becoming of being, but the separation implied in leaving behind or moving toward a "true" self. In both directions, either in the true self that one is trying to become, or the true self left behind, one is always displaced from this sense of imaginary identity. A "true self" thus creates nothing other than a continuous sense of separation from oneself and the world.

This is also the case in the sense of one feeling empty. Emptiness is a lack, a sense of not being complete, whole, or "fulfilled."[118]   In fact, the word fulfilled, which means "completed to perfection," works in sync with the metaphysics of completion itself. Not being fulfilled thus refers to the idea that there is such a thing as being complete.   Again, the unhappiness comes not from what one is doing in life per se, but

---

[118] Here I am referring to a type of fulfillment, or quest for fulfillment which seeks to fill itself by way of outside metaphysical sources such as truth, ground, certainty, etc. This attempt at fulfillment is in contrast to the "imperceptible fulfillment" discussed in the philosophy of Wolfgang Schirmacher. See section 4.6 for more on this difference.

from the relation to not feeling the plenitude of an imagined fulfilled completion – a completion always judged according to principles *outside* the becoming of self as such. The relation to this idealization of being creates once again a separation, a displaced sensibility in becoming, for the place of being always stands in relation to a hypothetical "fulfilled" or "unfulfilled" self. Feeling empty and the unhappiness of this sensation, thus manifests itself partially in the false logic that there is any such thing as being complete – or completed by means of an external and imaginary relation to a foundational truth or "true self."

What we have in both of these cases is a sensibility of separation, or what we can call a continued distancing or distance from an external authentic meaning. We have a type of (unhappy) becoming which sees itself always in relation to something beyond, something outside the continuous becoming of self and being. We live, in other words, in a world that has not only lost signification and stabilized meaning, but more importantly a world which still yearns for what it now lacks. This is what Nancy means when he speaks of the world perceiving itself "as a world of separation and pain."[119] What Nancy is pointing us toward is a notion of world which no longer has any meaning in the sense of stabilized truth, foundation, or absolute ground. In Nancy's words, "there is no longer any sense of the world."[120] After the "death of God" (Nietzsche) all foundational principles from beyond have dissolved, yet in mourning this loss, we have created principles which serve in and as substitution. We continue living in such a way that we are always in separation, always in relation to principles beyond becoming and the world. This separation and the unhappiness that follows, is a condition that will continue as long as there exists a relation to a metaphysical "beyond," whether this be in the form a completed self, true self, or what have you. Being separated continuously from oneself in becoming is a given, but a separation and distance from an entity or idealization beyond is unhappiness. Becoming in itself is a continuous scattering and separation; it is only in relation to a

---

[119] Ibid

[120] Jean-Luc Nancy, *The Sense of the World*, trans. Jeffrey S. Librett (Minneapolis: University of Minnesota Press, 1997), p. 4.

stabilized entity outside this world of becoming that we experience a lack or emptiness in being and existence.

Taking all of this into consideration, Nancy draws our thinking toward the opening left possible in a world without sense and absolute meaning. He points us to a "finite thinking" or "a thinking of absolute finitude: absolutely detached from all infinite and senseless completion or achievement."[121] It is a thinking which no longer orients itself in relation to a beyond, thus no longer yearning for anything other than the finite becoming of world. In this thinking there would no longer be the absolute separation of being from itself, the separation of becoming from an authentic self always beyond the self, and the unhappiness entailed in always feeling displaced, incomplete, and somewhat out of place. A finite thinking attempts to think the world as world, nothing more and nothing less. In the world there is becoming, and in the world there is an opening for a world which, as Nancy points out, makes and creates sense. This of course is quite different from a world which hitherto was given meaning and sense. The difference lies in the realization that the world no longer has a meaning from above or beyond, but a meaning from within the world as world as becoming. As Nancy says, "the world *no longer has* a sense, but it *is* sense."[122] For Nancy, world is sense and sense is world; it receives its meaning only in relation to itself as such, no beyond, and no absolute truth *outside* the movements of becoming. In fact, the finite world in itself creates, "generates,"[123] and produces meaning in its state of continuous becoming, a be-coming always open to the coming of other. As Nancy states:

> Sense, for its part, is the movement of being-*toward* [*l'etre-a*], or being as *coming* into presence or again as transitivity, as passage to

---

[121] Jean-Luc Nancy, *A Finite Thinking*, ed. Simon Sparks (Stanford: Stanford University Press, 2003), p. 27.

[122] Nancy, *The Sense of the World*, p. 8.

[123] Here I am referring to Wolfgang Schirmacher's notion of "homo generator." See Wolfgang Schirmacher, "Homo Generator: Media and Postmodern Technology," in *Culture on the Brink*, ed. Gretchen Bender and Timothy Druckrey (Seattle: Bay Press, 1994).

presence - and therewith as passage *of* presence.[124]

Meaning in this sense comes not from a world beyond, but from the becoming of world as such. Meaning comes not as a gathered unity from above, but as a singular difference from within the movement and "transitivity" of becoming. Nancy's call toward a finite thinking, a thinking of sense as world – a world where sense *makes* sense as compared to looking for sense from beyond, perhaps releases the world from the unhappiness and pain of absolute separation. What is necessary is no longer looking from a distance *at the world*, which already implies a separation from the world, but simply a being and becoming *in the world*. Perhaps here, in a becoming which moves only in relation to the difference in world, or, in the "transitivity" of being-with, the gap of separation is less of an abyss. With this in mind, we can perhaps shed the unhappiness of separation, and open ourselves to a becoming which becomes the production of possible meaning itself. As Nancy says, *"In this sense,* today anew it is precise to say that it is no longer a matter of interpreting the world, but of transforming it."[125]

3.4 Uncertainty and the Opening in Aporias

What will become of our world is something we cannot know, and we can no longer believe in being able to predict or command it. But we can act in such a way that this world is a world able to open itself up to its own uncertainty as such.[126]

- Jean-Luc Nancy

Life as such is uncertain. The transitory and contingent nature of existence folds (Deleuze) one generation into the next.

---

[124] Nancy, *The Sense of the World*, p. 12.
[125] Nancy, *The Sense of the World*, p. 8.
[126] Jean-Luc Nancy, "What is to be Done?," in *Deconstruction: A Reader*, ed. Martin McQuillan (New York: Routledge, 2001), p. 457.

Approximately every second in life, five people are born into this world and two depart.[127] Incessant movement and the continuous transformations of time expose a becoming which has no ground or permanence from which one can hold, stop, or posit, even for a moment, a stable identity within or outside the self. All things move toward becoming other in a constant transformative gesture without beginning or end. When one looks at a photograph of oneself as a child and then another photo of oneself in the time of now, one cannot help but wonder what activity occurred between the one and the other. The body not only transformed and is continually transforming, but the idea of self also seems lost in the vacuous cycle of becoming other. Memory tries to hold this identity together, but even this fails to sustain stability in the illusive transformations of temporal and spatial becoming. In fact, memory is at times nothing other than an attempt to create and maintain a sense of continuity and continuation, a sense of how one thing leads to another. It strives for a sequential understanding of what one was, is, and perhaps is becoming. Memory strives in a determinate manner against the incessant movements of temporal instability. It attempts to hold still, to fix, if only for a moment, a place outside the steady flow of the becoming of existence. But the world in its continuous flux disallows any sense of absolute permanence even in that of mind or memory. We all know how memories fade and how at times new ones emerge spontaneously outside of any effort or desire. In other words, we do not even have complete control over our memories. At times we take them and at other times they take us. Furthermore, very few memories, if any, can withstand the constant waves of time, where one event (memory) blends into another in the ongoing movement of temporal becoming. Perhaps it is best to look at a particular memory as that of a stone by the sea. The stone as memory may never completely disappear, but as the sea continuously, at each and every moment, throws wave upon wave onto the surface of the stone, it transforms its shape into something other. Each new shape is related to the shape which came before it; however, each new

---

[127] Statistic from http://www.overpopulation.org

shape is also something new, altered, and forever different from its predecessor. The same goes for us in mind, memory, and body. So we have in front of us and all around us a space of uncertainty – an uncertain relation to self and world, space and temporal becoming, all slipping endlessly through the mind, memory, and the objects from which our relation to the world is made possible. We live in a contingent subjective and objective world, without ground, relation, or measure. From here however we must still make our way. In fact, *creating* our way is perhaps the only way through this uncertain terrain.

In a short essay entitled "What is to be Done?" Nancy exposes us to the fundamental aporia that exists in this question in relation to living in a world without measure. We sense in front of us a necessary act or decision, yet, we simply have no means from which we can verify the legitimacy of one move compared to another. We stand alone, anxious, and suspended in an indeterminable space without absolute knowledge, absolute justice, or determined horizon. And yet, we must answer to a future, a "what is to be done?" which will take us from here to there. We simply cannot stop with our hands tied and allow one injustice after another to float by our being, nor can we call upon an absolute source or measure as a means for decision. Essentially, our contemporary situation in the world brings us before, as Nancy states, "a doubly imperative response" – a predicament where "it is necessary to measure up to what nothing in the world can measure."[128] We must act, yet this act cannot be measured or legitimized by such references such as absolute truth, justice, etc.

So from where does one pull, extract, subtract or what have you, the source of inspiration to make a decision? How does one not stand indefinitely in a deferred space of inactivity and indecision? For Nancy, the answer to the question "what is to be done?" is quite otherwise. The aporia of this question opens the space for invention – a movement that comes not from an absolute external source, but from the possibility of creating a world in the space between the either/or of any particular situation. What emerges from the aporetic uncertainty is not

---

[128] Ibid

inactivity but the possibility of change via invention and creativity. Uncertainty as such opens the space for an event to come, or a becoming differentiated from the either/or of determinable acts or decisions. To stand momentarily suspended outside the absolute demarcation and fray of binary difference is to allow the multiplicity and interstitial complexity between these poles to come to the surface. As Nancy suggests, between the resignation of "doing nothing" and the "doing something" because an absolute source tells us to, stands the potentiality inscribed in invention. With this of course, comes the anxiety of decision and movement without measure – a transition from here to there without reference and certainty as a guide. But, as Nancy says as he concludes his essay: "Where certainties come apart, there too gathers the strength that no certainty can match."[129]

---

[129] Ibid

Part 4: Fragments: Aporias, Anxiety, Uncertainty, and Nothingness

4.1 Indeterminacy: Nietzsche

> The metaphysics of the modern age begins with
> and has its essence in the fact that it seeks the
> unconditionally indubitable, the certain and
> assured [*das Gewisse*], certainty.[130]
>
> - Martin Heidegger

Nietzsche's philosophy is many things, but one fundamental aspect which pierces through the multiplicity of ideas, is the relentless pursuit toward an affirmation of uncertainty.[131] Constantly deconstructing notions such as ground, being, cause, effect, and so on, Nietzsche thoroughly undermines any sense of certainty in our relation to and with the world. In fact, one could say that Nietzsche's entire philosophical attempt at overcoming [*Uberwindung* as compared to *Umkehrung*][132] metaphysics is centered on breaking apart any sensibility toward the certain, assured, or that which stands firm as ground. Nietzsche's attempt therefore to overcome metaphysics is not simply an overturning of Platonism, as Heidegger would have us believe, but an attempt which is organized around a psychological, epistemological, and phenomenological relation to the notion of uncertainty. The world as contingent, fleeting, erratic in its constant movement and change, is the realm in which Nietzsche orients his philosophy.[133] He maneuvers through this difficult

---

[130] Martin Heidegger, *The Question Concerning Technology and Other Essays*, trans. William Lovitt (New York: Harper & Row, 1977), p. 82.

[131] This is a type of affirmative uncertainty which guides and motivates decision as compared to a passive notion which simply fluctuates *ad infinitum*.

[132] Here I am referring to Heidegger's placement of Nietzsche's philosophy as within metaphysics, or, as overturned [*Umkehrung*] Platonism.

[133] See Nietzsche's "description" of the world in aphorism 1067 of *The Will to Power*, trans. Walter Kaufman and R.J. Hollingdale (New York: Vintage Books, 1968), pp. 549, 550.

and anxious "terrain of the uncertain" never falling prey to the comforts of the indubitable. Furthermore, he manages this by creating/maintaining a perspectival and genealogical philosophy which always suspends or denies the dangerous satisfactions of absolute surety, absolute knowledge, and the comforts of metaphysical thinking.

It is by no means an easy task to suspend thinking in the space of the unknown. In fact, the anxiety of uncertainty always seems to pull or tempt thinking into the solid ground of the certain. Is it not easier thus to always desire a particular aspect of life, whether it be in our decisions, choices, or ways of experiencing the world, that attempts to give us a glimpse of the certain? Does espousing uncertainty as the backdrop to all existence, not run counter to all notions of pedagogy, where one is told from childhood to old age that sooner or later perhaps one may gain better insight into the world "as it is in itself"? In fact, Nietzsche's thinking is so radical in its deconstruction of all determined concepts and notions which seemingly guide us through life, that even when he reaches the limit point in his philosophy, his positing of the "will to power" as world, he steps back in hesitation and states "granted this too is only interpretation – and you will be eager enough to raise the objection? – well, so much the better."[134] Yes, for Nietzsche, an affirmative nod of so much the better. How can this be? How can Nietzsche reach the pinnacle of his own thinking, the place in his thought which for him perhaps comes closest to touching certainty, and still hold back and suggest that it may only be his perspective, his interpretation? He does so because it is the only way his perspectival philosophy can hold itself together. There simply is no room for the absolute, the indubitable, or the definitive space of certainty in the philosophy of life constructed by Nietzsche. His philosophy is thoroughly situated in the aporetic space of a perspectival and genealogical understanding of being/becoming in the world. It is aporetic not in the sense that there is no movement or transformation involved, but recognized as such because a thought never *passes through* and reaches the final destination of certainty. Simply stated, a

---

[134] Friedrich Nietzsche, *Beyond Good and Evil*, trans. R. J. Hollingdale (London: Penguin Books, 1990), p. 53.

concept, thought, or notion always stays forever suspended (albeit in constant transformation) in the restless space of non-passage (a-poria) and indeterminacy. For Nietzsche, any and all passage (*poros*) in thought occurs only on the level of value through the mechanisms of a will to power. There never is any movement or passage which crosses the uncertain/certain threshold.[135] The certain for Nietzsche does not exist, there are only degrees of active and reactive interpretations, or in his own words, "subtleties of gradation."[136] One may believe in the certainty of one's interpretation, but there is always a space (no matter how large or small) left open and indeterminate. This space left open is continuous because it is caught up not only in subjective indeterminacy, but perhaps even more importantly in the indefinite temporal and spatial gap of subject-object relations. In fact, any "relation" or "being-with" in general implies a certain degree of indeterminacy. In other words, the space-between is always shifting. Furthermore, the incessant change and flux of all phenomena (whether it be named subject, object, or thing) disallows any true stability or absolute form of certitude, for as something is coming to be it is also always already becoming other. Any attempt to move into the certain is always forced; it is always a gesture of closing out any other possible interpretations. All attempts at moving into and maintaining absolute certainty always contain an element of forced unity and closure - a desire to stop the movement and spacing of time.

We glimpse here the importance of maintaining quite the otherwise Nietzschean position, i.e., a temporal perspectival thinking which stays bounded in the aporetic space of uncertainty. To think outside this limit, in the realm of the certain, is an attempt to move outside the temporal and physical world, and into a transcendental world untouched by the restless movements of becoming. Thinking in the realm of the certain is

---

[135] In fact, for Nietzsche any and all forms of binary logic are false and need be seen as remnants of a metaphysical history – a pseudo-teleological history from which he no longer wants to be part. The "genealogical method" espoused by Nietzsche is fundamentally, at least in one respect, a deconstruction of all binary logic.

[136] Friedrich Nietzsche, *Beyond Good and Evil*, trans. R. J. Hollingdale (London: Penguin Books, 1990), p. 55.

nothing other than an attempt at not living *in* the world. As Nietzsche would perhaps say, this striving for the static form of the indubitable, is a hatred of life itself – a hatred of the transformative uncertainty of becoming. Two questions immediately emerge from these assertions: first, how is it possible to maintain a perspectival uncertainty without falling into mere relativism, and secondly, what determines the criteria or mechanism for such acts as decision, truth, and responsibility?

For Nietzsche, the answer to these questions revolves around the creative force of ongoing interpretation, opened up, exposed, and legitimized by the "death of God." This phrase represents the moment in history where thinking begins to turn away from the long history of metaphysical and transcendental truth. It is the time when thinking begins to turn not toward a construction of more absolute truths or legitimization of decision by measure of these "indubitable truths," but toward an unraveling of the very metaphysical truths that hitherto reigned. This moment could perhaps be recognized as a turn from attempts at constructing absolute truths to a desire to "deconstruct" the very historical grounds and foundations from which our modern times emerged. At the very least, the "death of God" pronounced by Nietzsche, brought with it an understanding that no truth stands outside of the historical/genealogical movements of time, and thus all truths are contingent and open to change.

This realization brought truth to a level of human desire, as compared to a truth situated in a transcendental or metaphysical realm of God or what have you. What should also be noted here is that the "death of God" not only exposes a world where truths and laws are no longer ordained by an absolute deity, but a world where the very foundations of truths in themselves no longer hold sway. In short, absolute truths are brought down (overturned) from the metaphysical stature of certainty to the domain of human participation, desire, and thus into the uncertain realm of human creativity. Nietzsche's genealogical (deconstructive) philosophy gives us a world less grounded and less certain, but simultaneously gives us a world where truth, ethics, responsibility, etc., must be continuously created. This continuous transformation (transvaluation) leaves each truth always open to future configurations, thus always uncertain and never completed in the form of totalization. As Alain Badiou would say, there is always an "unnameable" or part which is left open in the naming of a truth. The part left open releases truth from the totalized domain of being determined and absolute. An absolute truth attempts to close the ambiguous space from which change and movement may occur. It surrounds itself with the indubitable certainty of itself, thus it attempts to escape from the contingent, transient, and historical world, into the static realm of metaphysics. All attempts at absolute truth are thus nothing other than attempts at escaping the responsibility of being, deciding, and thinking in the historical and temporal world of uncertainty. In this world one must decide not from a pseudo-certain resource from above, but from the immeasurable and uncertain terrain of creativity. A decision must occur within the aporia of decision/indecision itself. Maintaining and enduring the indeterminacy of being and becoming in a world without measure, not only opens an infinite space of aporetic responsibility, but furthermore and most importantly calls one toward, as Derrida would say, a decision worthy of being called a decision.

4.2 The Nothing of Anxiety and the Anxiety of Nothing: Kierkegaard

> Innocence is ignorance. In innocence, man is not qualified as spirit but is psychically qualified in immediate unity with his natural condition..... In this state there is peace and repose, but there is simultaneously something else that is not contention and strife, for there is indeed nothing against which to strive. What then is it? Nothing. But what effect does nothing have? It begets anxiety.[137]
>
> - Soren Kierkegaard

---

[137] Soren Kierkegaard, *The Concept of Anxiety*, trans. Reider Thomte (Princeton: Princeton University Press, 1980), p. 41.

Anyone who has ever experienced the fundamental uncertainty of all things, knows that it springs not from a something, not from a fear, a pain, a sadness, an occurrence, or anything whatsoever that exists as recognizable and known. The anxiety of uncertainty senses only the absolute nothing, the pure nothing that spreads itself out as an infinite yawning abyss. The nothing is only sensed, only felt like a slight tremor upon the surface of the body. It has no depth, no structure, and no chronological temporality from which one can begin to describe its phenomenal touching upon ones being in the world. And yet, it is there, it is sensed as an open space between, a pure in-between without measure. Between what, one must ask? In short reply, between every-thing, an indeterminate space of nothing between each and every-thing. Its motions vibrate between the spacing of differentiation. The movement and space *between* all things (whether distant or slight) is the uncertain non-negotiable zone which begets anxiety. Nothing *is* the between, the uncertain spatio-temporal gap that exists in all difference. Between this-or-that is nothing because between this-or-that all things remain to a degree uncertain and unknown. Anxiety is situated (perhaps suspended is the better description) in this open gap of nothingness. This nothingness spreads in all directions, with no middle, no end, nor beginning. It exists as a zone where movement in itself is produced simply by the activity of decision and the re-organization of differentiation that follows. (Here is not the time to discuss Deleuze's philosophy of "the fold,"[138] but perhaps it is best to think of these movements, this re-organization in relation to decision and thus new configurations of differentiation as a folding and unfolding series of motions). One could call this zone of indeterminacy, this nothing where movement is the spacing of differentiation, the aporetic space of uncertainty. The aporia of decision, of responsibility, etc., exists because this gap of nothing, this zone of indeterminacy can never be filled. One simply cannot close the gap of nothing and uncertainty. In fact, any attempt at filling this gap or closing down the movements of constant change, and thus continuous variations of differentiation through decisions,

---

[138] See *The Fold*, trans. Tom Conley (London: The Regents of the University of Minnesota, 1993).

creates a negative force upon the very fabric of being and becoming *with* the world. Being-with is never static, and any attempt to make it so is nothing other than a perverse desire for closing down the movements of differentiation itself, and thus a fleeing into the non-anxious realm of absolute certitude. It also expresses a dogmatic desire for the One-All – an entity which fills all gaps, all spacing, and all differentiation. In short, this type of indubitable thinking wants to rid the world of the anxious, enigmatic and aporetic space between all differences – this "nothing" which keeps all relations ambiguous and uncertain.

It is important to stress here that this "nothing as between" or "gap of uncertainty" is not one entity which stands simply between two or multiple differences. The "differences" and the "nothing between" exist more so in a continuum or ambiguous flux, intimately connected with one another in the fabric of becoming. As Nietzsche states:

> Our usual imprecise mode of observation takes a group of phenomena as one and calls it a fact: between this fact and another fact it imagines in addition an empty space, it *isolates* every fact. In reality, however, all our doing and knowing is not a succession of facts and empty spaces but a continuous flux.[139]

We see first off that the movement into "fact" entails a grouping of phenomena and isolation. Furthermore, this delineation is not only from that of another fact, but from an "empty space" between them. This mode of successive thinking contains one sequence after another where one thing is always demarcated by that of another. It imagines that one thing or another is not always contaminated (to use a notion of Derrida's) by another. But this is never so. The "nothing" discussed above, which is the between of differentiation, is always touching the entities caught up in differential becoming. Furthermore, the entities (being that they are not isolated facts) are also always in contact

---

[139] Friedrich Nietzsche, "The Wanderer and his Shadow," aphorism in *A Nietzsche Reader*, (Harmondsworth: Penguin, 1977), p. 57-58.

with other entities. An occurrence or event, in fact, is perhaps nothing other than an interstitial crossing of multiplicities, where difference, decision, the spacing of differentiation, chance, and the uncertain nothing, all meet in a moment of becoming. The important point here is not necessarily what ingredients make up an event, but the understanding that all the variables mentioned touch, stay touching, blend, and constantly intermingle in a zone of indeterminacy.[140]   Again, to close down this type of movement and intermingling of entities, and to posit a dogma of binary opposition and certainty, is an attempt to shut down the uncertain and ambiguous nature of becoming. It simply wants nothing to do with the anxiety between differentiation, the "nothing" which holds it together, the touching entailed in being-with, and the interstitial place where they all meet from moment to moment in constant transformation. Yes, nothing begets anxiety, as Kierkegaard states, and the two notions together (interwoven, circulating, and at work in the becoming of being and world) open the space and disposition for events to come.   It is the nothing between every-thing, the spacing between multiplicities, and the difference or *différance* between all entities, which creates the incessant movement, novelty and change in this world.   It is of utmost importance therefore to maintain and nurture the anxiety by which this becoming of world takes place.

4.3 Affirmation: Nietzsche

> Nietzsche's "yes" is opposed to the dialectical "no"; affirmation to dialectical negation; difference to dialectical contradiction; joy,

---

[140] This "zone of indeterminacy" thus described is analogous to Nietzsche's description of the world as "will to power." Nietzsche's concept of "will to power," in my opinion, is an extremely insightful description of the movement of coming-to-be, or becoming as *event*. Again, the naming of the multiplicity of variables at stake seems to have less importance than the inter-activity, the no-outside, and the continuous anxious movement of forces at play in phenomenological becoming, or in this case, what I am calling event   See aphorism 1067 of *The Will to Power*, trans. Walter Kaufman and R.J. Hollingdale (New York: Vintage Books, 1968).

enjoyment, to dialectical labour; lightness, dance
to dialectical responsibilities.[141]

- Gilles Deleuze

Uncertainty carries with it the possibility of an obsessive desire for certainty. Intimately connected to this uncertainty is an ontological anxiety – a restless (Nancy) sense of being which at times yearns for the closure of certitude. In this state, any event left open and ambiguous (especially if temporally indefinite) creates a problematic demand to have answers where there perhaps are none to be found. In short, being unable to tolerate uncertainty, leads to a desire to close down the gap of uncertainty that exists between whatever entities are at play.

To give a simple example, let's say someone were to make a call[142] to a friend whom they had recently met for dinner. The friend does not answer, so the caller leaves a message. Let's say that the friend does not return the call. At first the caller would think perhaps that the message did not get left on the answering machine, so they would try again. After once again not hearing from the friend, the caller may begin to ruminate on their last meeting at dinner. They may think perhaps that they said something to upset the other, or, perhaps something was said out of place, or perhaps... and so on. The caller may also begin to wonder if the friend had perhaps left town, etc., etc. In summary, this process of "trying to know" may go on indefinitely, especially if the person being called never responds back. Soon enough, however, the caller's true desire changes from the original desire to talk with the friend into a much deeper desire to fill the gap of uncertainty which pervades over the entire situation. Now, they simply want *to know* what has happened - they want to be freed from the uncertain modality of perhaps itself. The "perhaps" is now the phenomenological obsession, not the desire to talk with the friend. A conversation

---

[141] Gilles Deleuze, *Nietzsche and Philosophy*, trans. Hugh Tomlinson (New York: Columbia University Press, 1983), p. 9.
[142] In retrospect, this metaphor would work even better here if one perhaps looked into the various ways in which Avital Ronell uses the notion of "call" or "calling" in her work.

with the friend is now substituted for a much larger problem, i.e., filling the uncertain gap of non-knowledge.

The example given here is obviously very simple, but the activity described may be applied to any phenomenological event where uncertainty is at play. As stated earlier, the uncertain gap that exists between any or all entities, if not tolerated, may lead to an obsession for certitude. This obsession may lead to many forms of knowledge and insight into any particular situation, but it will never lead to absolute certainty. Even if the friend (to go back to our simple example) finally replies back and says that they simply went on a long vacation, you do not know for certain that they are telling the truth. In any situation, or any event, there is always an indeterminate space, whether large or small, from which the notion of uncertainty expresses itself. Furthermore, any theory or philosophy of absolute truth and knowledge is always exposed to the never ending slippage that occurs when trying to hold together (through the *isolation* we discussed earlier) a concept as certitude. Any form of conceptual organization or forced identity (in order to grasp or understand) always leaves remnants of that which exceeds the attempted totalization. The excess is the trace (Derrida) of that which maintains difference in attempted unity,[143] and the maintained difference holds open the space of uncertainty.

So, what to make of this incessant gap of uncertainty? Nietzsche takes a novel approach to this situation. Instead of forcing thoughts, concepts, and theories into the futile space of metaphysical and transcendental certainty, he opens his philosophy to the uncertain – an uncertain not only as a backdrop from which a decision springs forth, but an affirmation of uncertainty as a relation to difference in itself. Nietzsche utilizes the active power of affirmation in the face of ceaseless uncertainty. He says "yes" to the ambiguous, enigmatic, aporetic nature of life, thus not only tolerating the uncertain, but moving it into a mode of joy and laughter. Nietzsche places the anxiety of uncertainty back where it should be; in the ontological space of being which precedes the psychological obsessive

---

[143] Here I am also referring to Derrida's statement that "the relationship of unity to itself implies some difference" as discussed earlier.

ruminations toward absolute surety. In fact, contemporary views on anxiety and obsession have a lot to learn from Nietzsche, for anxiety in itself is not the problem; it is the *symptoms* expressed in the intolerance and inability to sustain uncertainty itself.[144] The desire for certainty in relation to uncertainty creates the problematic symptoms the contemporary world now mistakenly calls anxiety. As Renata Salecl says in her interesting book on contemporary notions of anxiety, "Contingency might appear as horrifying but, in the end, what really produces anxiety is the attempt to get rid of it."[145] To view anxiety as a symptom is to miss the fundamentally positive potentiality of an ontological restlessness that precedes notions of decision and responsibility. Without this *a priori* anxiety, there in fact would be no such thing as a decision, for to make a decision one must first be held temporarily in the space of indecision.

The aporia of decision/indecision is thus intimately connected and structured around a notion of anxiety which precedes the symptomatic attempt found in trying to release oneself from the uncertainty at hand. Anxiety, before the attempt to get rid of it, is necessary in its ability to maintain and suspend aporetic thinking. If aporetic thinking, as I am trying to show throughout this essay, is an ethical way of thinking against the dogmatic pursuit toward certainty, then an anxiety which precedes the symptomology described is fundamentally one which should be nourished and resurrected from the negative domain of contemporary thought. The concept of anxiety should be re-thought and re-valuated for its essential contribution toward an ethical thinking – an ethics situated in the aporetic realm of uncertainty, becoming, being-with, and difference. Nietzsche's affirmation, his "yes" to this way of thinking, may bring his thought far from morality, but not from the possibility of thinking ethics. If there is a possibility, and I believe there is, for Nietzsche's philosophy to be thought in terms of ethics, it is likely to be found well beyond such notions as good or evil. Of

---

[144] I wish to note here that an aspect to my thinking throughout this essay is to re-think anxiety as a positive potentiality before it reaches the negative symptomology expressed in an inability to maintain uncertainty.

[145] Renata Salecl, *On Anxiety* (London: Routledge, 2004), p. 69.

course, the title of his book *Beyond Good and Evil* already points us in this direction.

An affirmation of uncertainty is one step in not only freeing oneself from the obsessive desire for absolute knowledge and truth, but an indispensable tool for maintaining the aporetic structure of decision and responsibility - a possible ethics to come. Nietzsche's affirmative yes to uncertainty as such, allows the restlessness (Nancy) of anxious becoming and indeterminacy a place within the realm of possibility, a move quite different than the obsessive quest toward absolute knowledge. Anxiety, if affirmed as possibility and potentiality, leads not toward suspended inability, but toward active decision-making and creative ability.

4.4 Anti-Dialectics: Nietzsche, Deleuze

> The anti-dialectical and anti-religious dream which runs through the whole of Nietzsche's philosophy is a logic of multiple affirmation and therefore a logic of pure affirmation and a corresponding ethic of joy.[146]
>
> - Gilles Deleuze

In a short essay entitled "Seven Variations on the Century" Alain Badiou names the seventh variation "anti-dialectical." The anti-dialectical is for Badiou a thinking of the singularity of the "Two" without synthesis. Between the Two, or the "we" and "what-is-not-us,"[147] there exists, what Badiou in a recent seminar at the European Graduate School named, "an experimentation of difference."[148] The "between" here is not a static entity that

---

[146] Gilles Deleuze, *Nietzsche and Philosophy*, trans. Hugh Tomlinson (New York: Columbia University Press, 1983), p. 17.

[147] Alain Badiou, "Seven Variations on the Century," *Parallax* (Routledge) vol. 9, no. 2 (2003), p.79.

[148] Alongside the possibility for an "experimentation of difference" there also exists, as Badiou describes in this essay, a possible antagonism which creates a "dialectics of the anti-dialectical." This occurs because "Either we see the what-is-not-us as a polymorphous formlessness, a disordered reality; or else we see it as *another* 'we,' an external, and therefore antagonistic, subject." My concern

simply holds the entities apart, but more so a spacing of difference itself – a spacing which generates movement and experimentation. In other words, the "space between" is experimentation itself – a movement which holds the Two in constant circulation. Here is not the place for a full analysis of Badiou's thinking on this, but for now it seems we can utilize his notions of "a Two without synthesis" and "an experimentation of difference" in better understanding the anti-dialectical "dream" (as Deleuze states) in Nietzsche's philosophy.

At first glance, Nietzsche's philosophy may seem caught up at times in nothing other than the movements of antagonism. Provocative in style, his texts *seemingly* (I emphasize this "seemingly" for reasons that will hopefully become clear) wish to perpetuate an already known style of thinking based on conflict, dialectic, and then perhaps even moments of temporary totalized resolution.   Furthermore, Nietzsche's interpretive philosophy seems at times to promote a type of dialectical thinking in relation to difference, where one entity stands in relation to an-other – a relation which stands as an opposition to overcome. But this is not so, for as Deleuze tells us, "Not all relations between 'same' and 'other' are sufficient to form a dialectic, even essential ones: everything depends on the role of the negative in this relation."[149] We see it is not the relation of difference in itself that creates the dialectic but the perspective from which the movement finds its manifestation. In the case of dialectics, it is the power of the negative (Hegel, Nancy[150]) which gives birth to its transformative becoming. As we have

---

here is to emphasize the possibility for an "experimentation of difference," for it articulates the uncertainty of the other as compared to a named and thus closed off other which simply promotes antagonism.

[149] Deleuze, *Nietzsche and Philosophy*, p. 8.

[150] See Nancy's book *Hegel: The Restlessness of the Negative*, trans. Jason Smith and Steven Miller (Minneapolis: University of Minnesota Press, 2002). In this book Nancy rethinks Hegel in a very interesting manner outside the usual reading of Hegelian dialectics. With this in mind, I still wish here to juxtapose the term *negation* (as that which promotes synthesis, homogenizing, etc,) and the term *affirmation* thus expressed in Nietzsche's philosophy.   As Deleuze mentions, it is important to see Nietzsche's anti-Hegelianism.   Whether Nietzsche is altogether correct in his reading of Hegel and the dialectic remains to be seen. Perhaps the negative without the dialectics of synthesis, etc., will show to be not that different from the activity of Nietzschean affirmation.

seen, Nietzsche's thrust in philosophy is his desire for continuous affirmation – an active affirmation which views the (Hegelian) negative as simply reactive. To move beyond *reactive* thinking is to see the difference of the Two (Badiou) as a space for *active* experimentation. If, on the other hand, one designs a philosophy of the negative as the propelling force behind transformation, the movement in itself will contain only a constant back-and-forth of reactive motions caught up in attempts at periodically synthesizing the ongoing experiments of the Two. Dialectics as such is by all means a denial of the other as absolute other, or an attempt at least periodically to merge the other into the same. It does not let the absolute differentiation stand as pure difference, for the negation in dialects usually implies a goal or concrete manifestation of temporary synthesis. For Nietzsche, difference in itself is enough, or as Deleuze states:

> In Nietzsche the essential relation of one force to another is never conceived of as a negative element in the essence. In its relation with the other the force which makes itself obeyed does not deny the other or that which it is not, it affirms its own difference and enjoys this difference.[151]

We see here a Nietzschean double affirmation of difference, for in the relation, difference affirms itself as other and at the same time does not deny the other its essential difference. Both ends keep their difference, and yet between the two there is movement and transformation, or again to use the phrase of Badiou, "an experimentation of difference." Experimentation here implies a continuous exchange, a simultaneous giving and taking from the other, but never a forcing of the other into the domain of the same. As with Nietzsche, the differences stay as difference, are affirmed as difference, and the activity of forces between circulate in a space uncertain or undetermined by the

---

[151] Deleuze, *Nietzsche and Philosophy*, pp. 8-9.

logic of recognition or sameness. The other recognizes the other as other, and vice versa.

This space for experimentation is not simply a solipsistic subjective relation to the other, nor does it imply, in its refusal for "communion" or merging with the other, that all things thus rotate in a subjective field of knowledge. It is quite otherwise. The maintaining of difference, in fact, allows a thinking of the other as other outside the self, whereas an attempted synthesis within the structure of difference always transforms the other into the same. Furthermore, the same entity, concept, or subject that always sees only the same in the other, stays also unaffected as same. To sustain difference is to hold and affirm the other as absolutely always other. It also means that there is always some uncertain space from which the "experimentation of difference" occurs. The desire to know the other in certitude is only an attempt to think the other as same. Again, the move into certainty always tries to close down the space of differentiation along with the anxiety of being an absolute other amongst other others. The quest for absolute certainty entails a negation of singularity. To affirm difference as it is, in all its uncertainty and lack of communion or synthesis, is to stay open to the possible unknown events, which continuously emerge from the aporetic space of activity within the between of differentiation.

But Adorno's *Negative Dialects* has also taught us that the concept of dialectics is so much more. He knows that to become "anti-dialectical" is not as easy as simply refusing the Hegelian notions of synthesis, mediation, resolution, teleology, progress, etc. In fact, in Adorno's complex style, he states:

> The task of dialectical cognition is not, as its adversaries like to charge, to construe contradictions from above and to progress by resolving them – although Hegel's logic now and then, proceeds in this fashion. Instead it is up to dialectical cognition to pursue the inadequacy of thought and thing, to experience it in the thing. Dialects need not fear the charge of being obsessed with the fixed idea of an objective conflict in a thing already pacified; no single

> thing is at peace in the unpacified whole. The
> aporetical concepts of philosophy are marks of
> what is objectively, not just cogitatively,
> unresolved.[152]

We see here, that no objective thing can be pacified by a
subjective thought, and no thought can ever cross the uncertain
abyss and entirely capture the thing being thought. The gap
between thought and thing is uncertain and as Adorno
insightfully notes, the aporias in philosophy thus mark this
unresolved terrain. It is important to stress that the aporias of
unresolved tension are not simply due to a faulty subject or
interpretation, but more so to the other thing which eludes
absolute totalized conceptualization. The concept cannot
completely surround or fill in the contours of an object. In other
words, it is not just a limit on cognition, but the instability of
thing-ness in the world of becoming and the relation to the
attempted conceptualization. Thing and thought stand not as
same but as difference itself – a difference promoting a ceaseless
experimentation.

4.5 The Nothing that Exposes Aporetic Being: Heidegger

> The indeterminateness of that in the face of
> which and for which we become anxious is no
> mere lack of determination but rather the
> impossibility of determining it.

> Anxiety reveals the nothing.

> The nothing itself nihilates (noths).

---

[152] Theodor W. Adorno, *Negative Dialectics*, trans. E. B. Ashton (New York: Continuum, 1973), p. 153.

For human existence, the nothing makes possible
the openedness of beings as such.[153]
                                    - Martin Heidegger

From the absolute indeterminacy of nothing, we are thrown
(Heidegger) as finite beings into this world. We emerge as
beings from nothing, not a nothing as no-thing,[154] but a nothing
understood as indeterminacy as such. It is the impossibility of
determinacy, not simply a lack of determination, as Heidegger
points out, that exposes us to the fundamental anxiety of being
thrown into the world. Unbeknownst to where we are going, and
from whence and where we came, we simply *happen*. One day
or moment we happen – we happen to come into existence. In
existence we continue to happen, a happening, a becoming of
being in ceaseless motion toward death, thus once again
continuously exposed to the pure indeterminacy of nothing.
What is fundamental here is the understanding that we happen
and continue to happen (becoming) in the movement of nothing.
As Heidegger states above, "The nothing itself nihilates." There
is a potentiality in the nihilating movement of nothing. Perhaps
this motion or push entailed in nothing is better understood if the
Heideggerian phrase "*Das Nichts selbst nichtet*" is translated as
"The Nothing itself noths" as done by Michael Inwood.[155] A
nothing that noths is a nothing that produces activity, a
movement of *nichten* or "to noth." We see here in this sense that
nothing is not no-thing, or simply a negation of some-thing, but
a positive and indeterminate force of transitive noth-ing
(*nichten*). From the movement of noth-ing we are thus thrown
into the world. Furthermore, in life, as the becoming of being –
in the indeterminacy, the step to step gap of always becoming
other, we continuously emerge and re-emerge through the
movement of noth-ing. And finally, in "being-toward-death" we

---

[153] Martin Heidegger, "What is Metaphysics?," in *Basic Writings*, ed. David
Farrell Krell (San Francisco: HarperSanFrancisco, 1993). In the order of quotes
listed: pages 101, 101, 103, 104.
[154] Also see appendix where Nancy speaks of the term "no-thing".
[155] Michael Inwood, *A Heidegger Dictionary* (Malden: Blackwell Publishing,
1999), p. 145.

are always already exposed to the noth-ing of which we will once again become. Being as such is thus surrounded at all times by the indeterminacy and uncertainty of noth-ing. This is why Heidegger states that "*Da-Sein* means: being held out into the nothing."[156] Anxiety, in the face of nothing, reveals being, not in relation to particular beings, but the being of being. Anxiety holds us out into the nothing; it exposes *Dasein*.

Further on in "What is Metaphysics," Heidegger points us to the double gesture of being exposed to nothing. On one hand, as mentioned, it reveals *Dasein*, or being which is not in relation to particular entities, and on the other hand, it "directs us precisely toward beings"[157] as particulars. In other words, the noth-ing of nothing discloses the being of being, and in another direction it moves us toward other beings. The movement toward other beings is a turning away from the anxiety of pure nothing. We cannot escape the noth-ing of nothing, but through the interaction of other particular beings we may perhaps repress or simply lessen the sensation of fundamental anxiety. Again, the noth-ing of nothing in anxiety does not cease, it merely disperses into various particular configurations that we may perhaps call worldly distractions. As Heidegger states: "The nothing nihilates (noths) incessantly without our really knowing of this occurrence in the manner of our everyday knowledge."[158] Nothing continues to noth and we continue to move in accordance or in response to this incessant activity. Heidegger here does not seem to suggest in a direct manner what one should do in the face of nothing, but he does tell us that a distortion of the "nothing" has misleadingly turned it toward meaning negation. For Heidegger this is a sign of repressed anxiety, for anxiety as such exposes the original movement of nothing, the place where nothing is noth-ing, not the negation of some-thing or every-thing.

Utilizing Heidegger's insights into the anxiety of nothing, we can here move into a further critique of the role of nothing and anxiety in our present time. But first, let us summarize the main

---

[156] Martin Heidegger, "What is Metaphysics?," in *Basic Writings*, ed. David Farrell Krell (San Francisco: HarperSanFrancisco, 1993), p. 103.
[157] Ibid, p. 104
[158] Ibid

points we have brought forward in Heidegger's thinking on
"nothing":

(1) Nothing is not no-thing or the negation of some-thing.
(2) Nothing is a noth-ing, in the sense that nothing noths.
(3) Nothing *is* indeterminacy as such.
(4) Nothing is a correlate to anxiety in the sense that they reveal
one another.
(5) Nothing and anxiety reveal *Dasein*, the being of being.
(6) A turning away from the nothing moves us toward particular
beings.
(7) A turning away from the noth-ing of nothing leads to a
nothing understood as negation.
(8) A turning away from nothing turns original anxiety into
repressed anxiety.

With these points in mind, let us now enquire where we in
our time stand in the face of nothing. What is nothing to us in a
time where most of life seems to occur in the absolute distraction
of particulars? In a radical turning away from nothing, have we
not made of life a commodity where one particular entity merely
leads to another in a form of relentless substitution? And
furthermore, what of time? Do we have time for nothing, or do
we simply fill the open space of nothing with some-thing, anything? It seems so. But this would not matter much if it did not
take away from the indeterminacy necessary for such things as
decision, responsibility, event, etc. Where is there room for a
true decision - a decision caught up in the aporia of simultaneous
indecision, when there exists only a mechanistic movement from
one thing to the next? In an attempt to flee anxiety and nothing,
one simply abandons indeterminacy altogether and moves into a
pseudo-realm of predetermined certitude. One's "decisions" do
not "endure the aporia" as Derrida would say, of possibility
within impossibility; the decision merely moves through the
realm of measurement and calculation. In fact, this form of
repressed anxiety in relation to nothing absolutely negates the
aporetic sensibility of indeterminate being as such. Pure
determinate being wants nothing to do with the nothing that

noths. This being wants nothing to do with aporetic and indeterminate being.

In a critical manner, I wish to suggest here, that it is of ethical importance to turn away (at least periodically) from the distraction of particulars and turn toward the fundamental anxiety of nothing. In the face of nothing we can perhaps think and thus decide in the temporality of hesitation. Not a hesitation created out of fear, but a hesitation as a prolonged moment of indecision within the aporetic structure of indeterminacy. From this moment of hesitation, a decision may occur, and thus also the responsibility of being in a world with others. A decision in the exposed opening of nothing creates the ethical possibility of being in the world. Furthermore, by turning away from the nothing of anxiety, we turn away from the opening of event, the opening of the absolute other to come. Here it may be noted that anxiety not only exposes *Dasein*, but it exposes us to the indeterminacy of being as such. Being in this sense is aporetic through and through. Being in the face of nothing - in the face of nothing in particular but indeterminacy is aporetic being. Turning toward the nothing and affirming the original anxiety of becoming through and with the movement of noth-ing, allows being a place within the event of existence. Using our terms, aporetic being, being as becoming and event means: "being held out into the nothing," a nothing understood as absolute indeterminacy.

But what holds us out into the nothing? What enables us to turn toward the nothing? Quite simply, what holds us out into the nothing is the affirmation of uncertainty as the groundless ground of being as becoming. It is to affirm the nothing from which we were thrown into being, the nothing from which we continuously become while being, and the nothing to come. In relentless affirmation, the anxiety of nothing becomes not a nervous or agitated state of being, but more so a state of bewilderment. It is only in the turn away from nothing, in the turning toward nothing as negation that anxiety manifests into a state of agitation. Anxiety, as Heidegger points out, opens us to the "bewilderment" of the uncanny (*unheimlich*). Here we are not agitated, but exposed to aporetic being as such. The fleeing from anxiety, whether by repression, distraction, or substitution of one particular to the next creates the nervous and agitated being we experience in today's world. Being held out into the indeterminacy of nothing gives us the true possibility that exists only within the fabric of impossibility. Here we have the possibility of responsibility within the impossibility of completion. We are exposed to the never ending and indeterminate nature of aporetic being. Instead of living in the determined passage (*poros*) and distraction of project to project, perhaps we should periodically look into the aporetic space of nothing – a space open to decision within indecision and the novelty of event.

4.6 Imperceptible Fulfillment: Schirmacher

> Homo generator realizes the hope and the angst of the post-Hegelian philosophers, a *Dasein* beyond metaphysics, a human being that needs no Being, no certainty, no truth.[159]
>
> - Wolfgang Schirmacher

> We are above all and irresistibly Homo generator, expressly [*eigens*] self-generating beings with willfulness [*Eigensinn*] and self-love [*Eigenliebe*], who in the enownment [*Ereignis*] of technology lead an artificial life. Such a life of complete responsibility does not make us lords or masters over other circumstances, but it does make us the anthropomorphic generators of such circumstances.[160]
>
> - Wolfgang Schirmacher

---

[159] Wolfgang Schirmacher, "Homo Generator: Media and Postmodern Technology," in *Culture on the Brink*, ed. Gretchen Bender and Timothy Druckrey (Seattle: Bay Press, 1994), p. 70.

[160] Wolfgang Schirmacher, "On the Inability to Recognize One's Inherent Flaws - A Critique of Science's Conception of the Human," chap. in *Lebenslust: Philosophy of Artificial Life* (New York: Atropos Press).

As becoming be-comes, or comes to be in "being-with," homo generator generates. In the movement of generating and generation, homo generator simultaneously, at one time, creates and is created. Each time in producing contexts from within this world for becoming, it furthermore exposes itself to the "to come" of the future. In generating, homo generator moves from within a context of ever shifting self-created possibilities, and in generation, it comes to be in a continuous relation to difference and other. In both cases, homo generator exists only in relation to the world as world. There is no "outside" of world for homo generator, thus its movement through life is not one structured or organized by external measure. As in the quote above, homo generator "needs no certainty, no truth."

In contrast to the homo generator, Schirmacher formulates the notion of "homo compensator." As its name suggests, it moves through life at odds with what Schirmacher calls "*Eigenmangel*" or "one's own inherent flaws."[161] The homo compensator works at all times in a futile attempt at overcoming (through compensation) the flaws inherent to its own being. It stands, in other words, always in a negative relation to itself and the outside world - negation to itself in the sense of having an internal flaw in relation to external or worldly pressures, and to the outside world as an entity to overcome. In short, the homo compensator always sees itself in relation to a hindrance, an obstacle outside its becoming and generating self, from which it attempts an overcoming in quest of an imagined completion. As Schirmacher says, "Homo compensator defines itself in dialectical differentiation from nature, always looking for a synthesis that unites nature and spirit [*Geist*]."[162] Seeing itself at odds with nature, homo compensator attempts a life always in relation to a beyond – an identity outside the very movements of generating and generated becoming. Homo compensator thus lives in the metaphysics of attempted certainty, a life in the imaginary realm of complete, stable, and absolute Being as such. It strives, in a never ending dialectical synthesis of overcoming, to reach a terrain of certainty and "perceived" fulfillment. Homo generator, on the other hand, lives a life of "imperceptible"

---

[161] Ibid
[162] Ibid

fulfillment – fulfillment not in relation to certainty or certitude, but more so uncertain and "behind our backs."[163]   What therefore does this mean?

In relation to the notion of imperceptibility, Schirmacher states:

> How both happiness and suffering are realized in my life must be imperceptible, yet can perhaps be conceived. An imperceptible perception alone can fulfill our artificiality, one related to silence, this most powerful motive of language. Constant in its absence, imperceptibility could hold out as fulfillment and even lend the chaotic and seemingly failed life a touch of lightness.[164]

As we can see, imperceptibility in life is certainly there, it exists, but the elements in life which are imperceptible can never exist in certainty. Fulfillment, the type which occurs in the imperceptible realm of being, occurs from within the generating space of world. It is a fulfillment which arrives (Derrida) – an arrival which exceeds the domain of absolute knowledge or certainty. In this sense, it is in contrast to the type of fulfillment we discussed in section 3.3 where attempted and thus "perceptible" fulfillment always fails in its relation to an imaginary external notion of completion. This "perceptible" form of fulfillment leads to nothing other than pain and unhappiness, for in a futile attempt at completion and certainty, the self always find itself separated from an idealization of itself. The homo compensator, in fact, suffers from this very form of separation and alienation – the pain of existing in the self created gap – the space between ideal being and becoming. This space of separation between an imaginary idealized "complete" self and that of continuous becoming creates the unhappy self who

---

163 See Wolfgang Schirmacher, "Homo Generator in Artificial Life: From a Conversation with Jean-Francois Lyotard," *Poiesis* (Toronto) 7 (2005), p. 87.

164 Wolfgang Schirmacher, "Art(Ifical) Perception: Nietzsche and Culture After Nihilism,"   http://www.egs.edu/faculty/schirmacher/schirmacher-art(ifical)-perception.html:

lives in the "*ressentiment*"[165] as diagnosed by Nietzsche. This unhappy being exists in the self hatred and resentment of not being or becoming what it imagines it should. With this in mind, we must therefore look toward the "imperceptible" fulfillment of the homo generator. In generating and generation, it comes to sense (Nancy) its meaning and thus its possible fulfillment, not in the recognized and determinate domain of thinking, but in a "finite thinking"[166] open to the continuous and uncertain coming of difference and other. Imperceptible fulfillment is thus the fulfillment which comes, arrives, and remains in the always already unthought and unrecognized space of a generating world of generation.

---

[165] Friedrich Nietzsche, *On the Genealogy of Morals and Ecce Homo*, trans. Walter Kaufman and R.J. Hollingdale (New York: Random House, 1967).
[166] For insight into this term see Jean-Luc Nancy, *A Finite Thinking*, ed. Simon Sparks (Stanford: Stanford University Press, 2003).

Part 5: Conclusion

> The actuality of the spirit constantly shows itself
> as a form that tempts its possibility but
> disappears as soon as it seeks to grasp for it, and
> it is a nothing that can only bring anxiety. More
> it cannot do as long as it merely shows itself.
> The concept of anxiety is almost never treated in
> psychology. Therefore, I must point out that it is
> altogether different from fear and similar
> concepts that refer to something definite,
> whereas anxiety is freedom's actuality as the
> possibility of possibility.[167]
>
> -Kierkegaard

Perhaps more than any other issue, albeit through varying interventions, what this essay attempts to think through or ask, is what does it mean, or could it mean, to live, as Kierkegaard says, in "freedom's actuality"? What does it mean to live a life of freedom in what he calls the "possibility of possibility"? Not just the possibility of one *particular* thing or another, as in choosing one (definite) thing over another, but the possibility of this possibility itself. In other words, what does it mean to live, act, decide, respond, etc., in the aporia of freedom itself, a freedom which on one hand opens us to the pure opening (Nancy) of possible possibilities, and on the other, leaves us no solidified mark or measure for pre/determined determination? In "freedom's actuality" we thus exist in an indeterminate space of knowing we must move forward, act, decide, etc., and yet, at the same time, we cannot call on an absolute authority, presence, or predetermined entity as a guide. Freedom as the absolute possibility of possibility, or simply the aporia of freedom itself, cannot call on such notions, for any attempt would resemble nothing other than a following or continuation of that which was already known. It would be a response or decision moving not

---

[167] Soren Kierkegaard, *The Concept of Anxiety*, trans. Reider Thomte (Princeton: Princeton University Press, 1980), p. 42.

through the aporetic terrain of non-knowledge and uncertainty, as Derrida points out, but through a path already made clear by a predetermined thought or horizon. Absolute freedom, in other words, opens us to a world without absolute measure. We stand thus in the opening of freedom - in the aporia of anxious indeterminacy. What we do here, or what we do in relation to the aporia of freedom, makes all the difference in regard to how the world unfolds.

With this in mind, there is of course no absolute solution to the antinomies we continuously confront throughout our lives. Finding an answer to the various aporetic occurrences within becoming would simply lead to a life closed down to the absolute freedom within being itself. In short, each time anew we must confront the aporias we face. Ethical possibility, or as Derrida would say, a decision worthy of being called a decision (and thus a "responsible" decision), exists only in this uncertain terrain of contextual becoming – a becoming which be-comes not through the determined path of absolute knowledge or truth, but through the opening (Nancy) in the aporia of being itself. Aporias open us to freedom, the possibility of possibility, the place where, as Derrida has taught us, an ethical decision may occur. Allowing indeterminacy to exist in our becoming allows a continuous coming to be with others – a becoming always open to the "to come" (Derrida) of the future. Aporias thus draw us toward the possibility of ethical becoming, the possibility of living an "ethical" life in a world without absolute measure - an ethics, in other words, of uncertainty.

Appendix: Email Correspondence between Michael Anker and Jean-Luc Nancy

Dear Jean-Luc,

Thank you for agreeing to answer some questions in regard to your work and philosophy. I have written up four sections (different but related areas of thought) for questions, and preceding each section is a quote or quotes from your various texts. The quotes serve, hopefully, to better contextualize the questions that follow them.

Section 1 – On Being Singular Plural

Two quotes from *Being Singular Plural*:

> Being cannot *be* anything but being-with-one-another, circulating in the *with* and as the *with* of this singularly plural coexistence. (p. 3)

> Being is singularly plural and plurally singular. (p. 28)

MA: First off, could you explain this notion of "being singular plural," and the difference, if any, between being singularly plural and being plurally singular. Furthermore, and in relation to the first quote above, do you use the phrase "circulating in the *with*" to emphasize being as a motion or movement (circulation), which is also a "spacing" in regard to the in-between implied in being-with? And lastly, is the notion "being singular plural" applicable to a potential thinking on politics or community (inoperative or otherwise)?

JLN: "to be" is not something, is no-thing: it is the event of "being"; this event is not one unique and common event for all beings; it is each time the event to be this or that; then, singular. But it is not unique for all, not even for the same individual – "I am" now, not the same as "I was" yesterday... Or it would be a unique "to be" for all, the event would be no longer event but something like substance.   Then, plural: here, "one" means necessarily one + one + one...

Section 2 – On Finitude

A quote from *A Finite Thinking*:

> *Finitude is the responsibility of sense*, and is so absolutely. Nothing else. And so I would also want to add: finitude is the sharing of sense. (p. 13)

And also a quote from *The Sense of the World*:

> Finitude is not the being-finished-off of an existent deprived within itself of the property of completion, butting up against and stumbling over its own limit (its contingency, error, imperfection, or fault). *Finitude is not privation.* (p. 29)

MA: Throughout many of your works you employ the concept of finitude, or at times the phrase "finite thinking." The term "finitude" in fact shows up in many different contexts, and therefore with many different descriptions. With this in mind, could you elaborate on what this term (finitude) means in relation to your philosophy? Also, in regard to the first quote above, in what manner is finitude related to a sharing of sense? And is a thinking on and in relation to finitude a "responsibility" as in a possible ethics?

JLN: Infinity means coming back to oneself absolutely, endless back to oneself: like an infinite line which comes back as a circle. Finitude means that this circle is broken and/or open. It does not close on/in itself. The break is: birth/death. The opening is: the same, as opening to a non achieved truth (or sense). Then, finitude opens in/as infinitude – to say, as (in)finitude, not as infinity...

But because "finitude" sounds negative or privative (it's finished! it's over!) it is perhaps better to say: absolute – that is detached (ab-solutum) – detached of any achievement and open to the infinitude of truth...

Section 3 – On Sense and World

A quote from *The Sense of the World*:

> Thus, *world* is not merely the correlative of *sense*, it is structured as *sense*, and reciprocally, *sense* is structured as *world*. Clearly, "the sense of the world" is a tautological expression. (p. 8)

And a quote from *Hegel: The Restlessness of the Negative*:

> Sense is the ideality of the sensible and the sensibility of the idea: it is the passage of the one in the other. Sense is thus total and infinite; it is the infinite relation to self of everything, the whole as such – which is to say, the relation to self of each and every thing, one through the other, for the other, in and as the other. (p. 49)

MA: In regard to the first quote above, could you explain what you mean by the world existing as more than a correlative of sense. In other words, are the two terms synonymous, and if so, do they lack any sort of relation or difference? As you say, they signify the same thing, but do they have a relation in the sense that they share a distance or spacing from one another? In short, is sense world and world sense, as within one another as immanent, or, is there a minimal difference or *différance* between them? This brings me to the second quote above, which speaks of sense as an infinite relation to self of everything. If the self and everything is immanently in the world as world and sense, does the movement and transformation of things in the world occur in a type of difference within a unity of world, self, and sense? Is this what you meant when you spoke of the movement in transcending during the EGS lecture in Saas-Fee, or when you mentioned the term trans-immanence?

JLN: The world is the spacing of sense. Sense is the circulation within the space. Like if you say: the world of Bach, this is a space, a disposition where one may go from that and that to that and that – from a musical feature to another one and to a religious feeling, to a climate, etc. This "going-from-to" is sense. The relation to self of everything is "difference," that is: does not achieve and close itself in itself. The "self" is each time one step further of... itself!

Section 4 – On Uncertainty and Openings

A quote from the essay "What is to be Done?":

> What will become of our world is something we cannot know, and we can no longer believe in being able to predict or command it. But we can act in such a way that this world is a world able to open itself up to its own uncertainty as such.

And a quote from the Introduction to *The Gravity of Thought*:

> If meaning depends on thought, insofar as it is thought that welcomes meaning (but does not produce it), then the meaning that 'dwells in what is open' depends on thought itself as opening. (p. 10)

MA: Many of your works rely on the notion of an opening, or open space, from which thinking may occur. What type of thinking occurs in this opening? Is it the type of thinking which orients itself around "maintaining [*garder*] the question" which you speak of in the essay "The Free Voice of Man"? Also, in regard to the first quote above, do you believe that this type of thinking (finite thinking?), or a "maintaining of the question" has the potential to open the world up to its own uncertainty as such? And, what would this imply for such notions as decision, responsibility, etc, since there is no ground or measure in the opening or open space of an uncertain world?

JLN: Precisely. We are responsible for the uncertainty of the opening, which maintains the world unachieved, uncompleted, without end, result or conclusion. This is more than maintaining the question. This is beyond the question: opening is beyond question and answer, or beyond affirmation and negation. In a way I would say: opening maintains the opening that is the form of opening, a mouth or a source or a sex or an open house.

What makes a work of art? It opens again the opening...

Sorry if I answer briefly... Your questions are very large – it drives me to go to the essential. Perhaps later I will be more precise.

Bibliography

Adorno, Theodor W. *Negative Dialectics*. Translated by E. B.
Ashton. New York: Continuum, 1973.

Agacinski, Sylviane. *Time Passing*. Translated by Jody
Gladding. New York: Columbia University Press, 2003.

Agamben, Giorgio. *The Coming Community*. Translated by
Michael Hardt. Minneapolis: University of Minnesota Press,
1993.

____. *Idea of Prose*. Translated by Michael Sullivan and Sam
Whitsitt. Albany: State University of New York Press, 1995.

____. *Means without End*. Translated by Vincenzo Binetti and
Cesare Casarino. Minneapolis: University of Minnesota
Press, 2000.

____. *The Open: Man and Animal*. Translated by Kevin Attell.
Stanford: Stanford University Press, 2004.

____. *Potentialities*. Translated by Daniel Heller-Roazen.
Stanford: Stanford University Press, 1999.

____. *The Time That Remains*. Translated by Patricia Dailey.
Stanford: Stanford University Press, 2005.

Auge, Marc. *Oblivion*. Translated by Marjolijn de Jager.
Minneapolis: University of Minnesota Press, 2004.

Badiou, Alain. *Being and Event*. Translated by Oliver Feltham.
London: Continuum, 2005.

____. "Beyond Formalisation: an interview." *Angelaki*
(Routledge) vol. 8, no. 2 (August 2003).

____. *Deleuze: The Clamor of Being*. Translated by Louise
Burchill.. Minneapolis: University of Minnesota Press, 2000.

____. *Ethics*. Translated by Peter Hallward. London: Verso,
2001.

____. *Manifesto for Philosophy*. Translated by Norman
Madarasz. Albany: State University of New York Press,
1999.

____. "Seven Variations on the Century." *Parallax* (Routledge)
vol. 9, no. 2 (2003): 72-80.

Beardsworth, Richard. *Derrida & the Political*. Thinking the
Political. London: Routledge, 1996.

Beauvoir, Simone de. *The Ethics of Ambiguity*. Translated by
Bernard Frechtman. New York: The Citadel Press, 1976.

Borradori, Giovanna. *Philosophy in a Time of Terror: Dialogues with Jurgen Habermas and Jacques Derrida.* Chicago: University of Chicago Press, 2003.

Butler, Judith. *Giving an Account of Oneself.* New York: Fordham University Press, 2005.

Caputo, John D., and Jacques Derrida. *Deconstruction in a Nutshell: A Conversation with Jacques Derrida.* New York: Fordham University Press, 1997.

Critchley, Simon, Jacques Derrida, Ernesto Laclau, Richard Rorty. *Deconstruction and Pragmatism.* Edited by Chantal Mouffe. London New York: Routledge, 1996.

Critchley, Simon. *The Ethics of Deconstruction: Derrida and Levinas.* Edinburgh: Edinburgh University Press, 1999.

Deleuze, Gilles. *Difference and Repetition.* Translated by Paul Patton. New York: Columbia University Press, 1994.

____. *The Fold.* Translated by Tom Conley. London: The Regents of the University of Minnesota, 1993.

____. *The Logic of Sense.* Translated by Mark Lester and Charles Stivale. New York: Columbia University Press, 1990.

____. *Nietzsche and Philosophy.* Translated by Hugh Tomlinson. New York: Columbia University Press, 1983.

____. *Pure Immanence: Essays on a Life.* Translated by Anne Boyman. New York: Zone Books, 2001.

Deleuze, Gilles, and Felix Guattari. *A Thousand Plateaus.* Minneapolis: University of Minnesota Press, 1987.

____. *What is Philosophy?.* Translated by Hugh Tomlinson and Graham Burchell. New York: Columbia University Press, 1994.

Derrida, Jacques. *Aporias.* Translated by Thomas Dutoit. Stanford: Stanford University Press, 1993.

Derrida, Jacques. *A Derrida Reader: Between the Blinds.* Edited by Peggy Kamuf. New York: Columbia University Press, 1991.

Derrida, Jacques, and Maurizio Ferraris. *A Taste for the Secret.* Translated by Giacomo Donis. Malden: Polity Blackwell Publishers, 2001.

Derrida, Jacques. "*Différance.*" Alan Bass. Chap. in *Margins of Philosophy.* 3-27. Chicago: University of Chicago Press, 1986, c1982.

Derrida, Jacques, and Bernard Stiegler. *Echographies of Television*. Translated by Jennifer Bajorek. Cambridge: Polity Press, 2002.

Derrida, Jacques. "Faith and Knowledge." trans. Samuel Weber. In *Religion*, ed. Jacques Derrida and Gianni Vattimo. Stanford: Stanford University Press, 1998.

_____. "Force of Law: The 'Mystical Foundation of Authority'." trans. Mary Quaintance. In *Deconstruction and the Possibility of Justice*, ed. Drucilla Cornell and Michael Rosenfeld. New York: Routledge, 1992.

_____. *The Gift of Death*. Translated by David Wills. Chicago: University of Chicago Press, 1995.

_____. *Margins of Philosophy*. Edited by Alan Bass. Chicago: University of Chicago Press, 1986, c1982.

_____. *Memoires for Paul de Man*. New York: Columbia University Press, 1989.

_____. *Negotiations*. Translated by Elizabeth Rottenberg. Stanford: Stanford University Press, 2002.

_____. *Of Grammatology*. Translated by Gayatri Spivak. Baltimore: Johns Hopkins University Press, 1976.

_____. *On Cosmopolitanism and Forgiveness*. London: Routledge, 2001.

_____. *On the Name*. Stanford: Stanford University Press, 1995.

_____. *On Touching - Jean-Luc Nancy*. Translated by Christine Irizarry. Stanford: Stanford University Press, 2005.

_____. *The Other Heading*. Translated by Pascale-Anne Brault and Michael B. Naas. Bloomington: Indiana University Press, 1992.

_____. *Politics of Friendship*. Translated by George Collins. London: Verso, 1997.

_____. *Rogues: Two Essays on Reason*. Translated by Pascale-Anne Brault and Michael Naas. Stanford: Stanford University Press, 2005.

_____. *Specters of Marx*. Translated by Peggy Kamuf. New York: Routledge, 1994.

_____. *Spurs Nietzsche's Styles*. Translated by Barbara Harlow. Chicago: University of Chicago Press, 1979, c1978.

_____. *Writing and Difference*. Translated by Alan Bass. Chicago: University of Chicago Press, 1978.

Dewey, John. *The Philosophy of John Dewey*. Edited by John J.
    McDermott. Chicago: University of Chicago Press, 1981.
Fathy, Safaa. *Derrida's Elsewhere (documentary)*. Brooklyn,
    NY, First Run/Icarus. 1999.
"Derrida's Elsewhere," transcript of documentary film by Safaa
    Fathy, <http://www.lrc.edu/eng/Derrida/Elsewhere.htm> (1
    October 2005).
Freud, Sigmund. *Inhibitions, Symptoms and Anxiety*. Translated
    by Alix Strachey. New York: W. W. Norton & Company,
    1959.
Heidegger, Martin. *Being and Time*. Translated by Joan
    Stambaugh. Albany: State University of New York Press,
    1996.
_____. *Contributions to Philosophy (From Enowning)*. Translated
    by Parvis Emad and Kenneth Maly. Bloomington: Indiana
    University Press, 1999.
_____. *Discourse on Thinking*. Trans. John M. Anderson and E.
    Hans Freund. New York: Harper & Row, 1966.
_____. *Nietzsche*. Translated by David Farrell Krell. San
    Francisco: HarperSanFrancisco, 1991.
_____. *The Question Concerning Technology and Other Essays*.
    Translated by William Lovitt. New York: Harper & Row,
    1977.
_____. *What is Called Thinking?*. Translated by J. Glenn Gray.
    New York: Harper & Row, 1972, c1968.
_____. "What is Metaphysics?." In *Basic Writings*, ed. David
    Farrell Krell. San Francisco: HarperSanFrancisco, 1993.
Hesse, Hermann. *Siddhartha*. Translated by Hilda Rosner. New
    York: New Directions, 1951.
Hutchens, B. C. *Jean-Luc Nancy and the Future of Philosophy*.
    Montreal & Kingston: McGill-Queens University Press,
    2005.
Inwood, Michael. *A Heidegger Dictionary*. Malden: Blackwell
    Publishing, 1999.
Kierkegaard, Soren. *The Concept of Anxiety*. Translated by
    Reider Thomte. Princeton: Princeton University Press, 1980.
_____. *Either/Or*. Princeton: Princeton University Press, 1987.
_____. *Philosophical Fragments*. Princeton, N.J: Princeton
    University Press, 1971, c1936.

Kofman, Sarah. "Beyond Aporia?." trans. David Macy. In *Post-Structuralist Classics*, ed. Andrew Benjamin. 7-44. New York: Routledge, 1988.

Levinas, Emmanuel. *On Escape*. Translated by Bettina Bergo. Stanford: Stanford University Press, 2003.

_____. *Otherwise Than Being, or, Beyond Essence*. Translated by Alphonso Lingis. Pittsburgh: Duquesne University Press, 1998.

_____. *Totality and Infinity*. Translated by Alphonso Lingis. Pittsburgh: Duquesne University Press, 1969.

Lucy, Niall. *A Derrida Dictionary*. Malden: Blackwell Publishing, 2004.

Lyotard, Jean Francois. *The Differend*. Translated by Georges Van Den Abbeele. Minneapolis: University of Minnesota Press, 1988.

_____. *The Inhuman*. Translated by Geoffrey Bennington and Rachel Bowlby. Stanford: Stanford University Press, 1991.

_____. *Peregrinations: Law, Form, Event*. New York: Columbia University Press, 1988.

Michelfelder, Diane P., and Richard E. Palmer. *Dialogue and Deconstruction*. Albany: State University of New York Press, 1989.

Mortley, Raoul. "Interview with Jacques Derrida." Chap. in *French Philosophers in Conversation*. London: Routledge, 1991.

Nancy, Jean-Luc. *A Finite Thinking*. Edited by Simon Sparks. Stanford: Stanford University Press, 2003.

_____. *Being Singular Plural*. Translated by Robert D. Richardson and Anne E. O'Byrne. Stanford: Stanford University Press, 2000.

_____. *The Birth to Presence*. Translated by Brian Holmes and others. Stanford: Stanford University Press, 1993.

_____. *The Experience of Freedom*. Translated by Bridget McDonald. Stanford: Stanford University Press, 1993.

_____. *The Gravity of Thought*. Translated by Francois Raffoul and Gregory Recco. Atlantic Highlands: Humanities Press, 1997.

_____. *The Ground of the Image*. Translated by Jeff Fort. New York: Fordham University Press, 2005.

_____. *Hegel: The Restlessness of the Negative.* Translated by
Jason Smith and Steven Miller. Minneapolis: University of
Minnesota Press, 2002.

_____. *The Inoperative Community.* Minneapolis: University of
Minnesota Press, 1991.

_____. *The Sense of the World.* Translated by Jeffrey S. Librett.
Minneapolis: University of Minnesota Press, 1997.

_____. "What is to be Done?." In *Deconstruction: A Reader*, ed.
Martin McQuillan. 456-457. New York: Routledge, 2001.

Nietzsche, Friedrich. *Beyond Good and Evil.* Translated by R. J.
Hollingdale. London: Penguin Books, 1990.

_____. *The Gay Science.* Translated by Walter Kaufman. New
York: Vintage Books, 1974.

_____. *Human, all too Human.* Translated by Marion Faber and
Stephen Lehmann. Lincoln: University of Nebraska Press,
1996.

_____. *On the Genealogy of Morals and Ecce Homo.* Translated
by Walter Kaufman and R.J. Hollingdale. New York:
Random House, 1967.

_____. *Thus Spoke Zarathustra.* New York: Modern Library,
1995.

_____. *Twilight of the Idols and The Antichrist.* Translated by R.
J. Hollingdale. Harmondsworth: Penguin, 1968.

_____. *Untimely Meditations.* Translated by R. J. Hollingdale.
Cambridge: Cambridge University Press, 1983.

_____. "The Wanderer and his Shadow." trans. R. J. Hollingdale.
Chap. in *A Nietzsche Reader*. Penguin classics.
Harmondsworth: Penguin, 1977.

_____. *The Will to Power.* Translated by Walter Kaufman and
R.J. Hollingdale. New York: Vintage Books, 1968.

Ronell, Avital. *Finitude's Score.* Lincoln: University of
Nebraska Press, 1994.

_____. *The Test Drive.* Urbana: University of Illinois Press, 2005.

_____. *Stupidity.* Urbana: University of Illinois Press, 2002.

Salecl, Renata. *On Anxiety.* London: Routledge, 2004.

Schirmacher, Wolfgang. "Art(Ificial) Perception: Nietzsche and
Culture After Nihilism." Http://www.egs.edu; Internet;
accessed 2006.

_____. "Homo Generator: Media and Postmodern Technology." In *Culture on the Brink*, ed. Gretchen Bender and Timothy Druckrey. 65-82. Seattle: Bay Press, 1994.

_____. "Homo Generator in Artificial Life: From a Conversation with Jean-Francois Lyotard." *Poiesis* (Toronto) 7 (2005): 86-99.

_____. "On the Inability to Recognize One's Inherent Flaws: A Critique of Science's Conception of the Human." Trans. Daniel Theisen. Chap. in *Lebenslust: Philosophy of Artificial Life*. New York: Atropos Press.

Sheppard, Darren, Simon Sparks, and Colin Thomas. *On Jean-Luc Nancy*. Warwick Studies in European Philosophy., ed. Darren Sheppard, Simon Sparks, and Colin Thomas. London: Routledge, 1997.

Tillich, Paul. *The Courage to Be*. New Haven: Yale University Press, 1952.

Unamuno, Miguel de. *Tragic Sense of Life*. Translated by J. E. Crawford Flitch. New York: Barnes and Noble Publishing, 1913, c2006.

Zizek, Slavoj. *The Puppet and the Dwarf*. Short Circuits. Cambridge: MIT Press, 2003.

_____. *The Parallax View*. Short Circuits. Cambridge: MIT Press, 2006.

CPSIA information can be obtained
at www.ICGtesting.com
Printed in the USA
LVHW091133140120
643545LV00001B/197